DISCARD

Helping Your Special Needs Child

Child

A Practical and Reassuring Resource Guide

SANDY TOVRAY
AND
MARIA WILSON-PORTUONDO

10/9/97
$10.99

Prima Publishing

*To Pepe, Maria Cristina, Jose Francisco, and to my
mother Adriana, for all their love and support.*

Maria Wilson-Portuondo

*To the memory of Dr. Judith Krieger Gardner, an
inspiration and guiding light, and to Tovah and
Rayna, each so very, very special.*

Sandy Tovray

Prima Publishing and its colophon are trademarks of Prima Commun-
ications, Inc.

Library of Congress Cataloging-in-Publication Data
Tovray, Sandra.
    Helping your special needs child : a practical and reassuring
    resource guide / Sandra Tovray, Maria L. Wilson-Portuondo.
        p. cm.
    Includes index.
    ISBN 0-7615-0011-1
    1. Handicapped children—Services for—United States—Handbooks,
manuals, etc.   2. Handicapped children—Education—United
States—Handbooks, manuals, etc.   3. Parents of handicapped
children—United States—Handbooks, manuals, etc.   I. Wilson-
Portuondo, Maria L.   II. Title.
HV888.5.T69   1995
362.4'083—dc20   95-3350
                                                                      CIP

95 96 97 98 99 AA 10 9 8 7 6 5 4 3 2 1
Printed in the United States of America

How to Order

Single copies may be ordered from Prima Publishing, P.O. Box 1260 BK,
Rocklin, CA 95677; telephone (916) 632-4400. Quantity discounts are
also available. On your letterhead, include information concerning the
intended use of the books and the number of books you wish to purchase.

Contents

Foreword   vii

Acknowledgments   x

Introduction   xii

1

Special Assignment   1

Who This Book Is For   7
Where to Keep This Book   8
How to Use This Book   8

2

Getting Organized   11

Record Keeping   13
Keeping Copies   15
Equipment and Supplies   17
Telephone Directory   24
Calendar   26
Organizing   28

3

Networking *33*

Rules of Networking 34
Getting Started 39
Networking Activities 41

4

Advocacy *53*

5

The Special Needs Child in the Medical World *65*

Before the Appointment 66
During the Appointment 73
After the Appointment 76
The Hospital Stay 80
Conclusion 84

6

The Special Needs Child in Education *85*

Before Starting School (Birth to Age Three) 87
After Starting School 87
Transition Services 104
Ongoing Tasks: Keeping the Child from
   Falling through the Cracks 105
Conclusion 114

7

Transitions   *117*

Daily Transitions   118
Major Transitions   121
About Transitions   123
Summary   155

8

Support Systems   *163*

Support Systems for the Child   163
Support Systems for the Parent   170

9

Special Siblings, Special Parents   *173*

The Interviews   175
Conclusion   203

10

Things We Never Even Thought About   *205*

Driving   206
Traveling with a Special Needs Child   207
Sexuality   210
When the Doctor Moves, Retires, or Dies   210
Moving away with a Special Needs Child   212
Money Management   216
Illness in the Family   217
Parents Aging or Dying   218

Socialization   220
After-School Care   221
Religious Rites of Passage   222
Dietary Restrictions   222
Housing   223
Occupation   223
Humor   224

11

Special Highlights   *227*

Chapter 2: Getting Organized   228
Chapter 3: Networking   230
Chapter 4: Advocacy   232
Chapter 5: The Special Needs Child in the
   Medical World   233
Chapter 6: The Special Needs Child in Education 234
Chapter 7: Transitions   239
Chapter 8: Support Systems   239
Chapter 9: Special Siblings, Special Parents   240
Chapter 10: Things We Never Even Thought About   240

12

Conclusion: Special Outlook   *245*

Glossary   249

Index   259

Laws and Resources   267

Foreword

As a practitioner in the field of special education in both the clinical and the school settings for over thirty years, I have observed the fears, anxieties, and confusion of parents who are trying to deal with the intricacies of the special education system. From the start, parents appear overwhelmed by a process in which they have had little or no experience or preparation. They are expected to meet with a group of professionals, all experts in their fields, who have observed and evaluated their child. They must follow discussions, understand reports, forms, processes, and unfamiliar terminology, and also agree to services of a highly specific nature. These issues only compound the anxieties that parents must face when their child requires special services.

My relationship with Sandy Tovray began when her daughter, Rayna, was referred to me for special education services. Sandy was already in the process of learning how the system works. She had spent years dealing with Rayna's physical disability and had only recently become involved with the educational aspect of the whole process. I came to realize that Sandy had done a great deal of research regarding the many aspects of special services. As the years of my involvement with Sandy and Rayna increased, I witnessed Sandy develop an even deeper sophistication in this area. She thoroughly researched all aspects of the process by staying informed, networking, reading, asking questions, and being involved with parent groups. Even with all the responsibilities of two daughters, having her own career, and dealing with the highs and lows of Rayna's disability, Sandy has been able to maintain a life that is rich and rewarding for herself and her family. As important as it is to take care of one's child, one must, as Sandy stated, "take care of oneself".

When Sandy and Maria came to me and told me they were going to write a book about helping special needs parents, I knew it would be a hands-on, practical, and reassuring approach to helping the special needs child. I had the good fortune of getting to know Maria Wilson-Portuondo at this time, both through meeting her and reading the personal stories throughout the book. I found Maria to be caring, responsible, and extremely open about her child's needs. Her stories reflect her courage, her struggles, and her successes in dealing with Maria Cristina's special needs. She takes a very direct, yet deeply emotional approach to dealing with Maria Cristina and I can see why success has come their way. Maria's stories will touch you and give you encouragement and support, yet practical advice as well. Her expertise as a teacher of and as a a parent to a special needs child makes it no surprise that Maria has been successful in her journey.

Together, these two dedicated mothers have compiled this manual for surviving special needs. Sandy and Maria wanted to share their knowledge of this process with other special parents in order to help alleviate fear and frustration. This book is their way of sharing their knowledge of the special education process and of helping special parents take care of themselves even while dealing with the myriad responsibilities that come with having a special needs child. Sandy and Maria impart a system that includes many aspects of organizing one's life in the "special education world". They provide detailed information on record keeping, note taking, advocacy, resources, and legalities. They include chapters on dealing with medical needs, developing support systems, and assisting the siblings of the special needs child. Through it all, these young authors, these mothers of special needs children, remind us that we are not alone. They've been through it and can help to smooth the road.

This book is a testament to Sandy and Maria's sincere concern for others. They have been able to survive the system through their own trials and errors, and freely share the knowledge that they have gained so as to alleviate some of this burden.

I am honored to include my thoughts in a book that I am sure will be a most valuable asset to parents. It is more of an honor for me to be connected with Sandy and her family and to count them as my friends. It was also a privilege to meet Maria Wilson-Portuondo and share her personal story. Special needs children and their parents will be one step further in the world because of the help they will receive from this book.

George Christopher
Special Needs Teacher
Memorial-Spaulding
Elementary School
Newton, Massachusetts

Acknowledgments

We first want to acknowledge our children, the ones with the special needs and their siblings. They are our source of strength and they are our inspiration. They give us the hope that fuels us to be the parents that we are, and they reward us, encourage us, and give us a sense of peace and fulfillment. Thank you Maria Cristina, Jose, Tovah, and Rayna.

We want to thank Prima Publishing for having the faith in our book proposal and the vision to let us go ahead and complete this book with all the fervor and commitment that we have as special needs parents. We need people to understand our emotions when we first go to an IEP, have papers given to us, learn new words, enter a foreign world, or when we don't know how to find a camp or an arts and crafts program, or how to sit in a doctor's office, or how to take care of the siblings and all the other little daily details that infiltrate our lives, our minds, and our hearts.

We also want to thank the participants in our interviews. They were instrumental in helping us put the personal touch on the technical aspects of special needs. Thanks to the professionals: Jean Harrison, Lisa Glassman, Janice Golden, Eileen Sullivan, Laura Perkins, Pat Kelly, Linda Wolf, Katherine Babbott, Judy Rothenberg, Sandy Alexander, Marie McDonnell, Eleanor Angoff; and thanks to the mothers who poured out their hearts and shared their private thoughts:

Joni, Jane, Judy, Alice, Ann, Karyn, Laura, and Ruth, and to the siblings who shared their feelings about their brothers and sisters. Without your invaluable input, we wouldn't have been able to put the personal touch to this very delicate and intricate subject. Thanks for sharing with all of us.

Thank you also to Andrea Shuman from the Department of Public Health and Dianne Curran, attorney at law, for assisting us with the federal regulations. And thank you to all the others who provided input in one way or another, including Mary Beth Fafard.

Sandy: I would also like to acknowledge Dr. Judith Gardner, posthumously. She was the inspiration for me to write this book. She encouraged me to put into writing what I had been sharing verbally with her. She was my daughter Rayna's psychologist for seven years, since Rayna was six years old.

I would also like to thank Richard K. Greenberg for all his wonderful support.

Maria: I would like to thank my husband, Pepe, for understanding my true need as a mother to put into writing all the emotions that I have experienced. I know that this book comes from his heart as well; I'm just the one to put it into written form.

We want to thank profusely and from the bottom of our hearts Mr. George Christopher for being so gracious as to write the foreword to this book. We thank him for his understanding and for his beautiful thoughts.

And finally, we want to thank all the special needs children in the world who have the courage and stamina to go forth despite the obstacles and to win the battle; or if not quite the victor, you at least put the best foot forward. Standing ovations and accolades to each and every one of you.

Introduction

In writing a book about special needs and how we as parents can better help our children, we acknowledge that there is a wide spectrum of needs within the field of special education. It runs the gamut from the most mildly affected, high-functioning special needs child to the child that is severely impaired and/or multihandicapped. In order to reach out to every special needs parent, we have aimed at gearing this book to as universal a reader as possible in the application of certain terms, definitions, and resources. Consequently, you might find certain sections less applicable to your particular situation and needs than other sections of the book. While every parent of a special needs child needs to know about evaluation meetings and IEP meetings, for example, not every parent has to deal with the medical world.

We wanted to create this book as a foundation for every special needs parent. We acknowledge that there are layers underneath that may need further exploration for certain parents. Parents of special needs children vary in a multitude of ways, and they are not homogeneous. The severity of the disability, the age and gender of the child, the geographic location, and the demographics of the family unit are all differing factors that are part of the makeup of a special needs child. There is also a wide variation of experience for you, the special needs parent. You might be a parent who has just been told that something is wrong with your child, and this is your first book on the subject, or you may be a more "seasoned" special needs parent, and this is your umpteenth book, your umpteenth search for information. Recognizing that some parents may need more in-depth information and support, we have also provided some resources that can help you investigate your particular needs further.

We have endeavored to cover this complex field by introducing as many aspects of special needs as possible, as well as providing you with some of the appropriate guides to further investigate your particular needs. While we can't address every specific special need, we can recommend some of the resources, whether a catalog, telephone number, professional, or organization in which to find this particular source. For example, you may have a Down's syndrome child, and although this book is not focused on that particular need, it does provide resources listed in the back that will help you conduct further research.

In keeping these generalities in mind, we also want to clarify what we mean by the term "special needs parents." While every parent isn't necessarily the biological parent of the special needs child, for expediency's sake we use the term "parents" to also include the surrogate parent, the single parent, and the guardian. And while special needs children include both the male and the female child, it is once again easier to refer to the special needs child as "he." Doctors and teachers also receive the male pronoun, but this is about expediency and not gender assumption. A final clarification includes the gifted child. While the field of special education extends to cover the gifted child, we have limited our text to address the special needs child within the other categories of special education.

In order to best help our child, we must understand a new language and terminology. Like any field or any subject, special needs comes with its own vocabulary. The more familiar you are with these terms, the better you will understand the concepts and be able to make decisions. When attending an IEP meeting, for example, if you hear terms such as "inclusion" and "least restrictive environment," and you are not sure of their meanings, then you don't have all the facts to help you make the proper decisions. Taking away some of the unknown in a field that is foreign to you can be the first major step in helping get through the process. If you need a support system, you need to decide who this source will be, for example, whether a social worker, a psychiatrist, or a psychologist. Knowing what each of these terms means can help guide you to the area you want to focus on and to the person best able to help your child, you, and your family.

We have written a glossary to highlight some of most commonly used terms that you may come across in dealing with your special needs child. We have kept this glossary as universal as possible. The particular specialty or medical problem that your child is faced with will probably have its own particular set of medical terms. We have provided resources at the back of the book for the different medical specialties. By writing to those organizations you will be able to gather information on the terminology specific to your child's medical disability.

The core of this text is based on in-depth research, personal experience as mothers of special needs children, and interviews with professionals in the field and other parents of special needs children. You will also notice that the word "handicapped" is not utilized in this book. In 1990, the Public Law 101-476 known as the Education of the Handicapped Act Amendment was renamed the Individual with Disabilities Education Act (IDEA), thus replacing the term "handicapped children" with "the individual with disabilities." And since an individual with disabilities is also referred to as a "special needs person," this is the term used throughout this book. The terms "special sibling" and "special parent" are terms we have chosen to refer to other members of the special needs child's family and are not to be taken as official terms.

In writing this book, we have endeavored to reach out to every parent of a special needs child to share our knowledge and personal viewpoints. A lot of information seems to be passed along by word-of-mouth, but we wanted to share our knowledge through the written word. Although we have divided the book into specific areas, such as the child in the medical world and the child in education, sometimes there are some crossovers in information. This repetition is sometimes necessary in order to convey some important steps in the process of helping your special needs child. For instance, remembering to bring the necessary papers to a meeting is a suggestion applicable to attending a school meeting as well as a consultation with a doctor. How to organize these papers is the crucial element, whether it is for the doctor or for the teacher.

As two parents of special needs children, we have interjected specific examples drawn from our experience into the main text. We believe that these examples will help illustrate some of the points we present and will also keep the book from being just a compilation of dry facts. We have also interviewed other parents to broaden our personal perspective and help you see the universal themes in the experience of being a special needs parent. This is what we believe makes the perfect blend for this book—the facts and the feelings.

Even though a child's special needs can easily become your main focus when contemplating the child's life, you don't want to overlook the fact that he is more than his special needs. For some children, their special needs may be a relatively small component of their life, for others a more prevalent part, yet each and every child is more than his special needs, more than his disability. We must not forget he is a human being, a future generation and a whole person, even while we recognize, address, and act on his special needs.

Special Assignment

Special is defined in the dictionary as "of a particular kind; distinct from others; not general." *Needs* is defined as "to be in want of." Combining these definitions, we arrive at a crude interpretation of special needs: "a particular kind, distinct from others, that is in want of." Legally, it is defined more specifically as any "instruction designed to meet the unique needs of a child in need of special education." On a daily basis, we as parents define special needs as extending into every aspect of the child's life—socially, emotionally, medically, and educationally. Everything in your child's life, every challenge and every accomplishment, will be special.

Though there is a legal definition for special education, this term is also defined by those who deal with it, such as parents, educators, advocates, administrators, lawyers, and anyone else involved in the educational process of the special needs child.

It is a common phenomenon for many people to have a narrow understanding of the definition of special needs, associating it with learning disabilities more than anything else. In reality, learning disabilities is just one of the categories that fall under the term. Also included in this definition of the special needs child is the gifted child. In addition, identifying special needs as learning disabilities may give the false impression that services are limited to children in the standard kindergarten through twelfth grade educational setting. In practice, special education services are legally granted to individuals from birth through age twenty-two, but the eligibility criteria varies in accordance with the different age levels and the definition of these different categories.

Federal law (Individuals with Disabilities Education Act) specifically mentions the following categories in its definition of special needs: mental retardation, hearing impairments including deafness, speech or language impairments, visual impairments including blindness, serious emotional disturbance, orthopedic impairments, autism, traumatic brain injury, other health impairments, specific learning disabilities, deaf-blindness, or multiple disabilities, and those who because of these impairments need special education and related services.

The federal regulations, in addition to specifying who is eligible for special education services, also specify that once these children are identified, they are eligible for "free appropriate public education," which means special education and related services are provided at public expense, under public supervision and direction, and without charge to the parents.

A child can be put on an education plan for any of the above needs. With laws and lawmakers involved in the decision making, there are many outside factors that can filter into this education plan. The teacher no longer solely makes the educational decisions for your child. No longer is one instrument or procedure acceptable to identify and classify a child as having special needs. With the establishment of evaluation and individualized education plan (IEP) teams, no one individual has the power to determine the future of the child.

The IEP also provides teachers and other service providers with a written commitment of the necessary resources that will enable a child with disabilities to receive special education and other related services. If the child is not making progress, parents can request that the child's IEP be reviewed to determine what modifications or changes need to be made to the child's program.

As parents of children with special needs, we have lived through the confusion and frustration that accompanies the realization that our children would experience their developmental years in a different fashion than we had imagined. We found ourselves inundated with terminology, experts, and documents that needed to be sorted out, sifted through, and eventually understood! Through ongoing conversations, we realized that we had similar questions, concerns, anxieties, and experiences. We quickly gained insight into each other's reality, which developed into a friendship, providing us with the opportunity to gain positive reinforcement from sharing our ideas and our hearts. Without realizing it, previous feelings of isolation and confusion were now being replaced with encouragement and support. We would share little anecdotes, "tidbits" and "how-to's," resources and experiences. We became each other's guide and sounding board. Although our children's special needs varied drastically, we discovered that we shared common threads: we've spent unsettled days followed by sleepless nights; we've imagined the worst; we've shed buckets of tears; we've had our hearts broken; we've worried about our child's future.

We both recognized that passivity would have to be overcome if we were to be successful in enabling our children to function in a world in which they are not quite in synch. Keeping the emotional factors intact and experiencing them at a different level, we would have to be active participants in order to facilitate our children's development. Our energy would have to be targeted in a positive way so that our children could best benefit.

In the beginning, one of the most difficult tasks that parents of children with special needs face is the realization that something is different with their child. There is a natural tendency to want to minimize the problem or even to deny that something is wrong. Identifying, accepting, and understanding the child's needs is the first step that must be taken in order to embark on this journey with your child. This in and of itself entails immense courage and strength, but there is another task that is even more challenging. We have to take on a new dimension in our parenting, with new roles and new responsibilities. As parents of children with special needs, we need to recognize that many hats need to be worn and many skills must be acquired.

We have been entrusted with a special assignment, thus we cannot afford to remain inert for an extended period of time to process the emotional implications of what has emerged. As a result of the child's diagnosis, we find ourselves immediately in the throes of executing what must be done. The practical and necessary tasks that lay ahead invade on the time that we need to process emotionally what has happened to our child. This process, while an important and necessary component, cannot impede on the time and effort needed to help the child. You must put aside personal fears or insecurities in order to pursue whatever it takes to support as well as enhance the child's future.

You don't necessarily proceed in a linear fashion, doing one thing first before moving on to the next step. You often have to proceed on a parallel process, working on the emotional implications while simultaneously taking action, even though you have not quite come to terms with it all. It is a time when parents are very vulnerable, confused, anxious, or angry, exacerbated by the realization that decisions must be made and action must be taken. Like so many tasks and challenges thrown our way as parents, this is a true juggling act, a search for the perfect balance.

Practical tasks can sometimes feel like a never-ending laundry list. From getting organized in the morning to wrapping up the day, and everything in between, it can all sometimes be overwhelming in its scope. The typical tasks that all parents encounter, compounded by the additional specific demands brought about by our children's special needs can lead to havoc if all is not properly organized. Learning how to channel and prioritize is an additional undertaking facing special needs parents. Children with language processing difficulties require more time and assistance in getting organized, or children with physical disabilities may need special apparatus, such as a brace, put on daily. Tasks such as these can lead to frazzled mornings, short tempers, and unintentionally raised voices, all ending in feelings of failure and inadequacy by the parent. Feelings of spousal and sibling neglect surface, adding to this sense of ineffectuality. In order to bring some order to this scenario, it is necessary to first acknowledge that these feelings are real, and then to be assured that they are not uncommon among special needs parents. Reaching out to others in the same situation can alleviate some of the feelings of isolation that may occur and bring you reassurance.

Torn between family demands and community obligations, you might feel that there just are not enough hours in the day. Achieving harmony in the family may require curtailing your expectations of yourself. The good intentions to attend the PTA meeting or volunteer for the bake sale may have to be postponed at certain times in the best interests of you, your child, and your family. Don't view this as a failure. Learning to prioritize and to draw boundaries is important; trying to "do it all" can be counterproductive. You need to conserve some energy to face the unexpected challenges and/or crises that sometimes crop up during your day. Our agendas are different than others in the community and we can no more compare ourselves to other parents than we would compare our children.

While you're striving to meet the demands and responsibilities so your child can reach his maximum potential, you may also be struggling with typical feelings of guilt and insecurity that can accompany the unwelcome diagnosis.

- Is my child's problem my fault?
- Am I doing all the right things?
- Am I really capable of advocating successfully for my child?
- Where do I begin?
- Who do I turn to?
- Do others feel the same, or am I just incompetent?

Overcoming guilt is not an easy task and it can lead you to inaction. Discovering that you are not alone in this sea of unknown, that you are not isolated in your situation, will clearly help abate these feelings. A more positive sense of self allows you to focus on the outside world, and it can often catapult you out of inaction.

Although this realization of what you are facing with your child, of what the short- and long-term implications of the diagnosis of your child imply, can be very frightening at the beginning, the more armed you are with resources and information, the less frightening and better enabled you are—thus, this book. We've been blessed with parenthood, yet burdened with extra difficulties. The road ahead is not fully mapped out. There will be many forks in the road, many unsettling moments of decision-making challenges. There will be periods of fears, confusion, and anxiety, but also times of hope, satisfaction, and celebration! One child's casual accomplishment may be another one's lifetime victory. Celebrate that victory, bask in its success, and treasure its accomplishments. Your child is unique with values to admire, dreams to help make reality, and a future to help shape.

This book is more than another information book about the special needs child; it is rather a working notebook that will help to keep the special needs parent on top of the situation and an active participant in helping the special needs child. It is meant to be read, reread, and written in. It is a potpourri of the many facets of the process of dealing with the special needs child, from a glossary of special terms to an inspirational support system in writing. It is our hope that this book will give you a source of encouragement and help you in becoming an active participant in the role of your special needs child, to make you the child's number one advocate.

Who This Book Is For

This book is for parents of special needs children; for anyone involved in raising and educating a special needs child;

for any professional dealing with special needs children to understand the world of the special parent.

Where to Keep This Book

Keep this book where it will be readily available to check for references and resources, whether addresses or telephone numbers, to put your hands on that information needed immediately, to refer to the glossary when a new word confuses you, to help organize yourself so you will be better equipped to handle your child, or just to know you are not alone out there without support. We include a chapter called "Special Highlights" (Chapter 11) to use as a quick reference and checklist after reading this book, so that you can quickly refresh your memory without having to search through every page.

How to Use This Book

- Read the book cover to cover
- Refer to different chapters for information and inspiration
- Read the parent interviews as written peer support
- Read the educational professional interviews to help with transitions
- Refresh your memory by rereading a chapter when the time is appropriate, for example, just before an IEP meeting
- Refer to a telephone number or address for resources
- Look up a confusing term
- Use the information to get and stay organized
- Refer to "Special Highlights" (Chapter 11)

This book has a twofold purpose: to give you basic information to guide you through the special needs process, and to provide you with a stepping-stone to help you create your individual personal directory. After you create your own calendars, telephone directories, and file systems, then you can make it meet your own individual needs and add as many or few telephone numbers as you need. Update your papers, your resources, and also future needs, checking your special calendar for short-term and long-term dates. As you use this book on an "as needed" basis, you should reflect more and more of your personal experience, reality, and contacts, thus creating your own special needs directory. But, most important of all, you should use it and make it your yellow pages, your resource book, your bible. Eventually, each book will be personally enhanced by you, the parent.

We, the parents, are the bridge between the many worlds of the child, from the medical to the academic to the world of life itself. We have been called upon to be strong, to have courage, and to be best prepared to help our child cross those bridges. We have beautiful, special children, and we are the special parents. They have their challenges to face, and we have ours. They have their tasks, as we have ours. They have their special needs, and we have our special assignments.

2

Getting Organized

"**S**pecial needs" is an umbrella term. There are some children who are diagnosed as a special needs child, go through the process of an evaluation, have an IEP designed and implemented, and that's the end of that. Perhaps at the most, follow-up meetings are arranged to assure that all is running smoothly. Then, there is the other extreme, where a special needs child experiences a constant stream of doctor's appointments for physical and/or psychological evaluations, hospital stays, or there are problems with the education plan, which almost ends up in court. And in between, there is a wide range covering many levels and degrees of needs. The intent of this book is to reach each and every one of you, to give you help, from those with the most moderate to the very severe, to the ones who never hit any snags and to those who are constantly meeting obstacles. For some, you might need to devour every word to help you get through it all. For others, after reading these chapters, you might need to extract one or two facts that apply to individual situations. In whichever case, you still need to be organized, know the terms, and be armed with as much knowledge as possible.

Discovering that there is a problem is only half the battle; dealing with all that it represents is the other half of the battle. You find yourself overwhelmed with emotions, questions, an endless list of "what if's" and "what do I do about's," new vocabulary words that need to be defined, and papers—papers to sign, papers to read, test scores, and IEPs. You find yourself jotting down a telephone number of a special *this* and an expert on *that,* a good source for *this*, and a great place to take your child for *that.* You open up your mail, and a new report is sent to you. "Sign this and return." "Keep this for your records." "Suggested follow-up testing—six months."

If you can't figure out how to do what with whatever, you feel lost. This does not translate into a controlled feeling to help your child. The overwhelming feelings and emotions now include feeling buried among the papers and confused about what to do with all this new information pouring into your home, your desk, and your life. You may feel like you are swimming in a sea of confusion, frustration, clutter, and helplessness. You will find in the end that organization is the key to unlocking some of the many frustrations you are faced with and to at least eliminate that part of the problem.

Most, if not all, doctor and school appointments are usually followed by a report, letter, etc. It's important to keep all these reports. The best thing you can do for yourself and your child is to get organized and stay organized, get on top of the situation and stay on top of the situation. You need to put your energies into the academic, emotional, and social ramifications of your child's problems, and not to tearing your house apart looking for that important document ten minutes before the IEP meeting or jotting down a reminder for testing in six months and then forgetting where you wrote it. The sooner you unclutter your life and establish a secure record-keeping system, calendar, and telephone directory, the better prepared you'll be to move on with all the proper steps enabling you to do the best you can for your child. Let's start by talking about record keeping.

Record Keeping

Keeping a separate section for everything related to your child's special needs is crucial. In the long run, it doesn't matter what system you use; the important thing is that you *use* a system and that it works for you. If you're the kind of person who likes to keep everything in a shoe box marked "Billy's Special Needs Materials," and you're comfortable with that, then do it. It doesn't make sense to tell you that there is only one system, because that isn't going to help you be organized. We do the best with the loose-leaf system. We have found through the years that this system keeps us the most organized, it is the easiest to keep up to date, and it is the easiest way to "put our fingers on" whatever we need as quickly as possible.

We encourage you to keep all your information in one area, including all your papers, resources, phone numbers, etc. This might help you to be organized. With subject dividers to separate the different categories, you can be fully equipped to be organized. It's as if we are in school taking a course, and we are prepared for our *special assignment*.

Sandy: My daughter Rayna has a multitude of special needs, spanning from medical to educational. The first thing we did is set up three different sections, one to keep all medical letters and information, etc., the other for academic materials, and a third section for miscellaneous materials. We further divided each section into subsections. For example, in the medical section we had doctor reports and therapist reports (occupational and physical); another subsection had the psychology tests and reports. We divided the academic section into IEPs, test reports, and teacher evaluations. The medical and the academic sections each had a miscellaneous subsection to cover any reports, letters, and information that didn't specifically fit into any category.

The final section was general miscellaneous, for information that didn't seem to gel anywhere. Basically, that is the least filled section, because the better you can divide up the information, the easier it is to find. Each section has blank paper in the front to jot down any information we would want to work on later. For instance, if someone mentions the name of a great camp that the child will be old enough to go to in three years, then I would put that information in the front of the miscellaneous section. (I would also cross-reference it in the telephone directory, to be discussed later in this chapter.)

Besides categorizing these papers in different sections, it is also advantageous to place them chronologically and put the dates in bold letters on top of the various reports. That way, if only one particular time is requested, it is easier to find that report if it is identified on top with the date. Also, you might want to identify the school year, so that it is also readily visible. For instance, if you want to refer back to your child's IEP for the third grade, you don't have to take the time to figure out what year that was; if you have both the date and the grade level marked, then the information is a lot more readily accessible.

My notebook looks something like this:

1. Medical: Doctor Reports, Letters
2. Medical: Therapist Reports, Letters
3. Medical: Psychologist Reports, Letters
4. Academic: IEPs
5. Academic: Tests, Reports
6. Miscellaneous and General Information

Your notebook might only have a very small section assigned to medical issues or a very small section for academics, therefore, your notebook should be organized to reflect your child's issues. For some of you, an accordion file might work better than a notebook. What you choose to use is not as important as the fact that you keep your papers organized and accessible.

Keeping Copies

Sandy: I was so pleased at finally organizing all the papers. I felt as if I could think more clearly and had a "handle on the situation," especially when I was looking for a new physical therapist and was asked for any back reports. How easy it was to flip to the section on therapist reports, to *copy* the reports, and to send them to the new person.

Never, we repeat, *never* send anything out to anyone, without keeping a copy for yourself. One of the most luxurious items in our house is not the wide-screen television or the microwave, but the copy machine. What a wonderful invention. Our advice to those who don't own one is this: First, always ask for two copies of a report (you can file them together and mark "COPY" on top of one); second, think about investing in a copy machine. There are many on the market today that are small and inexpensive. You don't need one that is going to do fancy things for you, you just want it to give you a copy. It will save time and energy and probably money in the long run. Remember, you need your energy in so many other areas. Whatever you can do to simplify your life, do it.

If owning a copy machine is not in the realm of possibility and you need to copy a report, at least make two when you get out to the copy store, so you can save time the next time that you may need the same report. If you are copying at a public place, do not leave the material to be picked up at a later date. Stay there while the copies are being made. If the person makes any mistakes during the copying process and needs to discard some of the copies, request that they be given back to you. That way, you are assured that no papers with your child's name that contain private and confidential information are floating around. You also protect your child's privacy by making sure that others do not read this information. One other advantage to staying on the premises while copies are being made is to assure that nothing gets lost or misplaced. And don't forget, even if a report is not two-sided, you can ask to have copies made back-to-back by feeding the same paper back into the machine and copying the second page of a report on the back of the first page. This will save you space in your notebook and help the environment as well. Lots of reports come two-sided already, and you can copy them the same way. But the key word is *copy*.

Equipment and Supplies

Because of our positive experience with the usefulness of technology, we highly recommend arming yourself with as much office equipment as money and space will allow. It would be helpful to have an answering machine, copying machine, fax machine, and computer (at least a typewriter or word processor). We also think a beeper and a car phone could be beneficial in getting and staying organized. We are not stating that it is a must to own every single one of them, but we recommend that you give it some thought, because they might be helpful in alleviating time-consuming tasks and eliminating some of the disarray that can occur in your life.

Maria: I have had the advantage to have at my disposal a wide array of office equipment in my home, because my husband needs it for his work. Some of this office equipment has turned out to be very beneficial in getting organized and in somewhat simplifying my life.

If you have to prioritize due to budget restraints, or because you wish to limit the amount of gadgets in your life, we think the first thing you may want to consider is the beeper. If you leave a message at a doctor's office, or if the school or your child needs you, then you are available to get a message no matter where you are. It also gives you and your child a sense of security, knowing you are always reachable. This can have its disadvantages as well, if not properly channeled. You don't want your child ending up with a crutch that blocks her independence. But, when used for the right reasons, a beeper is invaluable. How frustrating to leave a message with a school or a doctor, then have to sit home and wait for the call. Sometimes the secretary can give you exact information when the return call will take place, and other times you get answers of a more vague nature. In either case, you are a free agent to go about your business if you have a means for being reached outside the home.

If you can go on and be able to own more helpful aids, we would recommend the copy machine in your house. This will free up so much time and eventually will pay for itself. You need to be available for so much else, why not have the convenience of a copy machine. Next on our list then, would be the answering machine. The reason we put the beeper first was for those who could only choose one, you could bypass the machine and be always available on the beeper. But, if you can go for both, it's so easy to tell a school or doctor, "Just leave the information on my machine if I'm not home." You can also use it as a message center for yourself and your family. For example, if you know that you are going to be late and no one is home yet, you can call home and leave a message on the machine. That way, you can call when it's convenient and know that the family member returning home can pick up the message upon returning.

Sandy: I was once at an appointment with my daughter and I knew that the baby-sitter could stay until five o'clock. I also knew the sitter had taken my other daughter to the park. The appointment was running late, but I had a break and ran to the phone, called home, and on the answering machine left instructions as to what to do about dinner and where to drop off my other daughter. Another alternative, if I didn't have the machine, would have been to page her, give the return phone number at the appointment, and have her return the call. I would have done this if I didn't have the machine or it was an emergency. But, to have her pull over and find a phone to call wasn't really warranted in this case, so I used the convenience of the answering machine. See how the beeper serves as the number one item for convenience! Even with leaving a message at home on the machine, I also knew that the sitter could page me if she had any questions. (Car phones are also very helpful.)

Another way that you can use the answering machine is as a message center for yourself. That's right, call yourself. Although you may always carry a little notebook for writing down any information, it's just as easy to call yourself and leave a message on the machine to do something crucial when you return home.

Sandy: A doctor once asked me to send him Rayna's IEP from school, so I jotted this information down in my notebook, but to make sure I did it as soon as I got home, I called myself to remind me to do it when I got home. Then, when I was picking up messages, I simply heard my reminder, went right to the file folder, extracted the necessary papers, _copied_ them on my machine, and sent them off. Although I try to be diligent to check my notebook for anything I wrote down during the day, I can get distracted and forget. This way, my reminder was waiting for me when I got home, as a backup measure.

An additional advantage to having an answering machine is to allow it to pick up the telephone and record messages for you, even if you are at home but in the middle of something and you don't want to be disturbed. Perhaps your child is in the middle of a serious discussion or is having a difficult time with some homework, and you just don't want to be disturbed. These are optimum times to allow the message to be recorded, yet you should always be in earshot of the machine, in case it's an emergency. We are all so conditioned to grabbing the telephone when it rings and it may be difficult to not answer the phone, but with the answering machine you have the security of the machine recording the message, enabling you to "screen" the caller and, if need be, interrupt the message and pick up the telephone. This way, you can give your child 100 percent of your attention and return the call at a later time when you have finished with your child's agenda.

At a time when you are trying to consistently follow through on a routine, an answering machine allows you the freedom to shut out the outside world for a given period of time without losing important messages. Although it is imperative to teach our children to be flexible in life, that variables do play into routines, and that we must be able to meet changes when they occur, it is nice to be able to have a choice in answering the telephone. In the evenings, it allows us to read to our child, finish an activity, and put him to bed without constantly being interrupted. It allows for some quiet time for tending to the day. It also helps to stagger some of your phone calls so you are not overwhelmed with calls if you are physically or emotionally in need of some respite.

Maria: When the children were younger and Pepe was traveling, I came to see the telephone as a problem. I would be in the middle of explaining a homework assignment or Maria Cristina would have finally gotten herself organized to work on a task, when the phone would ring.

This interruption would interfere with the flow of things, and Maria Cristina would get very annoyed if she had to wait for me to finish talking in order for her to receive the help she needed to continue with her work. Getting children with special needs organized and started on homework can be difficult, because this is not a task that they find pleasurable or easy. Having the task interrupted by phone calls and other irrelevant stimuli can turn the homework time into chaos. Maria Cristina made it clear to me that she found the interruptions from telephone calls frustrating. Once we decided that we would not answer the telephone during the time allocated for homework, it became much easier to deal with the homework. Maria Cristina could no longer attribute all of her frustration to the telephone call interruptions, so we were able to hone in on some of the real difficulties inherent in the task she was involved with.

A valuable tool to have is call-waiting. This allows you to use the telephone while keeping it free for any other calls. How frustrating to call a doctor, to be told you'll get a call back, and then be afraid to use the telephone the rest of the day while you anxiously await the call. Call-waiting, if available in your area, allows you to be on the telephone and also receive incoming calls at the same time. The service involves a minimum charge, and it is worth it. A second line is also an option so that you can leave one number for the telephone call to be returned and still use the other phone line. Call-waiting is preferable and less costly. That way, you only need one answering machine as well.

The next priority on our list would be the computer and/or typewriter. We realize that many homes have at least a typewriter if not a computer, but some do not, and if you are going to be writing a lot of letters, they are invaluable tools. Another added benefit of having a computer in the home is the built-in dictionary and spell-checking feature found in most word processing programs, which can be very helpful for children with learning difficulties. By making the writing process less tedious, the child is free to concentrate on the creative aspects of education. With so many school systems implementing the use of computers in their programs, having a computer at home can also enhance whatever programs are being taught at school. If at all possible, buy a computer that is compatible with the computer system at school, to facilitate the school-to-home transition. With a home computer, both the special needs child and the special parent can benefit.

One other helpful piece of office equipment is the fax machine. The fax machine is not a must, since there are more inexpensive ways to mail information quickly, however, it might be beneficial to some as it can save time and running around.

Sandy: I truly believed a fax machine was not a necessity and that the *few* times I might *ever* need it, I could use a public one. Well, the expression "What did I ever do before I had . . . ?" certainly was applicable here. I ended up buying one and have sat in the convenience of my home and faxed letters to schools, permission slips to doctor's offices requesting transfer of information, and many other papers. And guess what—I don't even have to copy these documents before faxing. They never leave the house!

The last priority on our list is the car phone. Car phones can be costly, but if used judiciously, the expenses can be kept to a minimum. We believe that the biggest advantage to a car phone, besides the security of being able to call for help in an emergency, is calling ahead if you are late for an appointment. Also, if you are lost, even though you did your homework and obtained the directions ahead of time, you can call the office and ask for directions. Although, as we discuss in Chapter 5, it is essential to allow enough time to reach a designation, variables do filter in. Unexpected traffic can make you late, for example, and the anxiety level as you watch the cars creep and crawl while the clock seems to tick faster can be enormous. A car phone lets you call the office and let the secretary know your situation, so everyone can relax more. Let the secretary know exactly where you are and how long you anticipate the delay. Perhaps the next appointment after you is there, and you can switch. Always carry the phone number of your destination with you.

To review, here's our list:

Beeper
Copy machine
Answering machine
Call-waiting or a second line
Typewriter and/or computer
Fax machine
Car phone

We would also suggest that you keep a stock of mailing supplies in your house. Some supplies to always keep are white business envelopes, stamps, large manila mailing envelopes, two-day mailers, return receipt cards, and labels. That way, if a document needs to be mailed, you have everything at your fingertips ready to go. Also, store envelopes such as two-day mailers in the house (the post office will gladly give them to you). You can prepare everything at home before going to the post office, saving you time and hassles.

Telephone Directory

Remember that great camp that was recommended to you? Write it down, put the telephone number down, write the person who gave you the recommendation. Know where to find it when you want it. Here are some important tips to keep in mind when writing down phone numbers.

When noting a doctor's name and phone number, do not forget to write down the doctor's specialty. You might think you'll remember who the doctor is, but if he is someone you don't see that often, and if you have many different specialists that are all part of your yearly agenda, then you could easily forget which doctor is which.

It is also good practice to write down the name of the person who referred you next to any resource you enter in your notebook. Sometimes you will be asked who referred you. Also, it allows you to follow up and thank the person for that lead. In addition to the person's name, identify the resource so you know why you are calling that person.

Sandy: I keep two telephone directories, one for friends, family, etc., and the other for professional numbers. This makes finding the numbers I need to call much easier. I also use a loose-leaf type rather than a bound type, because it is easier to delete and add pages. Sometimes people move or change phone numbers, or you change therapists or doctors, and it's a lot easier to redo one removable page than to have a lot of crossing out and outdated telephone numbers. I also use a pencil or an erasable pen when writing them down, so if it's not a major change, I can just erase the number and write the new number. Sometimes, when I'm in the process of networking, for instance, finding a program for my child, I will sit with a big piece of paper, writing down all the telephone numbers, and then tuck that whole paper in the directory. (More about networking in Chapter 3.)

Keeping telephone numbers up to date and organized makes it quicker for you to find the number when you need it, and it cuts down on frustration. We recommend taking your directory with you to a doctor's appointment or IEP meeting. More often than not, a doctor or teacher will say that he needs to get in touch with your general physician or the guidance counselor, and it's a lot easier to whip out that book than to say you'll call the office later and give them the number. Also, if a recommendation for seeing someone is given to you, you can write the number down immediately. If you can't put the number in your telephone directory immediately, write the number on a sticky pad (most offices have these) and put it in the front of the directory or tape it on if you are afraid the paper won't stay sticky. The doctor or educator or whomever your appointment is with might recommend a specialist and might want you to call, so you can take the number right then and there.

Calendar

The last part of getting organized is having a calendar that is dependable. By dependable, we mean one that is easily accessible and one that will make sure you know what you are doing when. It is of no value to stick something on a calendar that you will never notice, or worse yet, forget to check. Having it readily available, like everything else, is essential.

Many times, we have been given long-term appointments or have been told to call back in six months. We turn to that particular month and write across the top of the page, "Call Dr. Smith for appointment." So, not only will we remember to call back when we should, we don't have to worry about forgetting. Like the phone directory, a calendar should accompany you to all appointments.

When writing down appointments, in addition to writing the person's name, write down who the appointment is for. Sometimes more than one family member may need to visit this person, so it's important to write down which family member has the appointment.

Sandy: Both my daughters had to see the same ophthalmologist, and I neglected to write down which daughter had which appointment. I almost brought the same child twice, forgetting what I had done. Now, in my calendar, I write the appointment, and which person has that appointment.

If you have a big meeting coming up, write yourself a reminder a week or month before the meeting to provide yourself with an opportunity to gather your thoughts and collect any relevant information from other sources that you may need. By doing this in advance, you are able to start writing down your questions. Always look at your appointment book or calendar at the end of the day, to make sure you are not forgetting something important, and then at the beginning of the following day, to see what is ahead. This may sound very overwhelming with all you have to do, but just a quick glance at your calendar will keep you abreast of what you have to do. It's always better to have things written down so that you are not kept awake at night suddenly wondering about the next day.

Maria: On more than one occasion, at the end of a hectic day, I have glanced at my notebook and noticed a task or phone call that I need to do before the day is over. Had I relied on my memory, I would have overlooked something important, which would make things harder down the road. At the end of the day, when you're tired, it is very easy to forget things, since you just want to call it a day. I have made it a habit to check my appointment book in the evenings and in the mornings, shortly after getting up.

Writing down appointments is not the only thing you should write in a calendar. If you are told by a source to telephone them on a certain date, put this in your calendar as well. That way you are not searching all over the place for the different parts of your day. Treat making a telephone call as a type of appointment, something you have to tend to that day. Another thing you can write in your calendar or appointment book is a reminder of messages you need to give to your child/children or spouse. Sticky pads can be helpful in this manner.

Organizing

Maria: At the start of the day or the evening before, I look at my appointment notebook and transcribe the information onto a sticky pad that I have divided into three sections: things to do, appointments, and telephone calls. During the course of the day, I can quickly glance at the sheet and have a clear idea of what still needs my attention.

It's always important to prioritize your agenda for the day. If you are swamped with too much to do in one day, take a good look at your list and consider the following options. First, can you move anything from today's list to another day when you are not so busy? If the answer is yes, don't just cross it off your list; make sure you write it onto another day in your calendar. Second, can you organize what you have to do in a way that helps you maximize your efforts and helps you to be more efficient? For example, if you're running errands, you can organize your destinations so that you follow a logical route rather than backtracking or going around in circles. If you are making telephone calls, decide which ones will be quick and short and which ones will require more of your attention. Though some appointments or tasks in your agenda will need to be addressed on the day and time scheduled, you need to be clear on what can be renegotiated with others and with yourself. You can create and negotiate your own agenda in many ways.

Being organized will help you keep it all together. There will be many days, even weeks, when you will have nothing to do in relation to your child's special needs. And then there will be times when you will be spending many hours in a day addressing an issue or an area in relation to your child's needs. Being organized and prepared will help you in those times when you are faced with a busy agenda.

Organization entails not only office supplies but also other means with which you can better organize and free up your time. There comes a time when you have to acknowledge the fact that you can't do it all—it's okay to delegate tasks to others and to relinquish some responsibilities to other people. By delegating tasks, not only will you be better organized, but you'll be more available to help your special needs child as well as other family members.

Delegating responsibilities can also have the added benefit of fostering independence in your child. By giving appropriate tasks to your child, ones that won't be too difficult and that can be accomplished without added stress, your child will feel good about himself, boosting his self-esteem. If he knows the task he is doing will really help you, he'll feel useful and needed. He'll feel like a contributing, successful member of the family, with you appreciating his help.

When thinking about ways to free yourself, consider the following questions:

- Do you need to look for a car pool?
- Do you need to look for a mother helper, baby-sitter, day care, or respite care?
- Do you need help with the housework or other alternatives if this is not financially possible? For example, can you share with your spouse or other family members some of the chores? Can you get any outside help? Can you exchange child care with someone so that you can be free to do some uninterrupted housework, get to the supermarket, or just spend

some time with the special needs child or the special sibling?

- Have you made some fun time for you? It's so easy to get so caught up in the daily routines, demands, and stresses of life that you can sometimes lose sight of necessary down time and leisure time that will relax and rejuvenate you to be a better parent to help your child. Go for a walk, read a book, get out to a movie, or just sit alone.

- Is there anything in your routine that you can let go of for the time being? For example, you could assign a time limit on the housework you will do or reassign the time by which you will finish a task. Take a breather before cleaning the dishes in the sink, etc.

- Are you doing too much? Do you need to pull back on some activities to conserve energy and increase stamina? If the mornings are chaotic and you are always rushing out the door late, then perhaps you can prepare the night before: set the breakfast table, make the lunches and store them in the refrigerator, lay out your child's clothes, etc.

How you choose to manage your time is not necessarily the way another person will. You have to discover what works best for you, but also listen to what others are doing. Perhaps it has never occurred to you to make lunches the night before or have the book bags packed and waiting by the door or put sticky notes on the dashboard of the car so you don't forget to do something that day. You might indeed gain a lot of skills and ideas from other parents to make your life smoother. It is always important to get support from other special needs parents, but when it comes to organizational skills, anyone can guide you. Just do what works best for you, listen to others, sift through the suggestions, experiment, and end up being the best organized, most relaxed parent there is!

Teaching children organization skills is a crucial part of preparing them for their life journey, so that they can start to fend for themselves. You can teach your child organizational skills in a variety of ways. For instance, many preparation strategies and organizing skills can be put into place to reduce the stress in the morning before school. The child can take an active part in some of the tasks for school preparation, including breakfast choices the night before, clothing choices, and getting book bags ready and notes to be signed. Other strategies for keeping things running smoothly can be to move the clock ahead or use the timer to remind kids of different tasks. With older kids, you might tell them that homework is not considered done until it is packed away in the book bag ready for school the next day. In this chapter we have addressed the importance of being an organized parent so that you may better help your special needs child. In addition, teaching your special needs child these organizational skills is a gift for a lifetime.

3

Networking

Though we tend to associate the term "networking" with the business world, it has its applications in the special needs world as well. Although it may have different interpretations in this area, the basic concept remains the same. *Networking* is defined as the exchange of ideas and information. One is trying to achieve a goal by exchanging, seeking, and gathering information, resources, and ideas. Imagine an intricate net in which the seeker of the information must find his or her way in order to reach the answer at the end. Another image is fishing in a large sea where one may not be able to see the fish, and using the net as a means to secure the catch. Networking is clearly an essential skill to have to be most effective throughout our children's journey. For some, it is a skill that comes naturally; for others, it comes with more difficulty, yet it can be successfully developed.

Networking, by its very nature, forces you to climb out of the isolating shell that may have initially enveloped you with the original onset of the diagnosis. That original sea of unknown that you thought you had to cross alone now has definition to it, with directions and many resources along the way. As you start gathering information and breaking through this isolation, you start putting in place what is helpful and saving or storing what isn't useful at the time.

While not necessarily a complex skill, networking is a skill that can be easily acquired and grow in strength, capability, and ease. You can start with some basic steps, and as you do more and more, you become more adept until it becomes second nature. These steps are not overwhelming at their inception and can lead to some very positive results. As we get further along in the chapter, we will give you some advanced steps that will make this skill more intricate. But for the novice, it is better to take successful small steps than to jump into an area that you are not yet comfortable with.

Rules of Networking

We have discovered some basic rules that have allowed us to make this process more tangible, thus allowing us to better understand the process.

The first rule of networking is never to throw away any information, no matter how inconsequential or useless it may seem at the time. Organize it, file it, store it away, consolidate, but never throw it out. You never know if it might be useful at a later time. If you can't use it, someone else down the line may be able to. And those very people will be the ones to have just the perfect information for you. Filing, sharing, and exchanging information is pivotal. Besides the fact that it is very exciting to discover resources or information that can be of help, it is also very satisfying to be able to reach out to others. Networking is a give-and-take process. Since resources, services, or contacts change over time, it is through the ongoing exchange of information that we often get to update and expand our pool of information. And that's just the first rule.

Next, remember that if a source that is suggested to you doesn't materialize into what you were looking for, don't just give up on that source. There are no dead ends in networking—that's our second rule. Finding a source that turns out not to be what you are seeking doesn't mean you have hit the end of the road. Like a maze, it just means a little backtracking and rerouting to find your way out, seeking a different direction. But at least it's a stepping-stone. The first thing to do is ask the person if he or she knows anyone else who can help you get to where you want to go.

You may also discover that even though this source isn't what you were originally looking for, it may be able to offer you something that you had never even thought of or even knew existed. It might not necessarily be of immediate help but is something to put away for later. For instance, you may call an organization because you were told they had an adolescent support group only to find that they don't, or that it is not what you are looking for, or that they meet on days that you can't attend. But you may discover that they service adults over twenty-one. Put that information away, because your child will be that age someday, and that source may be just the one you will be seeking at that time. It's not the end of the world if you don't save this information, but it can certainly make your life a little easier if you have already started the process of networking for this aspect of your child's life. You might, in fact, also utilize this source when the appropriate time comes and find that it wasn't of any consequence after all.

This moves us into the third rule: Follow every lead, no matter how inconsequential. There are times when a lead might seem inappropriate, and only later do you find out that your reaction was based on erroneous assumptions and lack of information. Sometimes the name or the location of a school, program, or organization can be misleading. As you gather information and talk with administrators, you may find that this lead may be what you are looking for after all.

It is important never to forget that you are your child's best advocate. You are the one out there fighting, campaigning, and searching the ends of the earth for your child. It is essential to always be active in this. Thus, the fourth rule: Always be active. You are the primary tool in networking. Opening yourself up to the world, asking questions, seeking answers—these are the skills that will get you where you and your child need to go. People need to know what you want if they are going to help you. Making people aware of your needs is the next step to having those needs addressed and hopefully answered. You don't know who is going to have the perfect answer for you unless the question is posed. No one can offer you the perfect summer program unless they know you are looking for one. A silent world is not the world that will best service your child. And don't be afraid to ask for help, to let other people assist you in your search, activating their resources and aiding you.

If you keep these basic rules in mind, you will always be in a better position to network and help your child. Remember:

1. Never throw away any information.
2. There are no dead ends in networking.
3. Follow every lead, no matter how inconsequential.
4. Always be active.

Ready? Let's apply these rules.

Networking encompasses an extensive list of activities, each one not necessarily mutually exclusive of the other. These activities often have a domino effect. As you put the system in motion, you will find that one thing leads to another. You have set a whole series of actions in motion that can lead you to some interesting places and to some unexpected discoveries.

The following activities all encompass the basic steps of networking:

- Finding various organizations
- Accessing medical personnel
- Finding educational programs
- Finding after-school and summer programs
- Finding support services (group counseling, tutors, occupational therapists, etc.)
- Finding peer groups (for the parent as well as the child)
- Finding transportation
- Preparing for the future
- Securing respite care or baby-sitters

There are many tools or resources to help accomplish these activities, some more obvious than others. A list of these tools might look something like this:

- Know what the organizations service and how they can best help you.
- Get on mailing lists.
- Speak up.
- Follow up on a lead.

- Stay informed through reference books, publications, and the media.

- Tell a friend that you need help (finding swimming lessons, for example).

- Look through the telephone book for possible programs or organizations.

- Browse in bookstores, particularly ones within universities that have an education department and teach courses in special education.

- Attend a course that is an introduction to special education. This is a good way to familiarize yourself with the field.

- Ask special education teachers for names and addresses of catalogs. On these mailing lists, you often come across new books, materials, or equipment that might be necessary or helpful for your child. Often, teachers are sent trade magazines and catalogs that target teaching professionals and school systems.

- Attend lectures or presentations offered by the special education department of your school system, by community centers in your area, universities, or by various organizations related to the special needs field. For many parents, attending topic-related presentations is difficult enough, let alone remotely related topics. However, even if you don't feel that the presented topics are your top priority, think about occasionally attending as an opportunity to network, meet other parents, and perhaps get a chance to chat briefly with the speaker. Through these interactions, you may discover leads to other talks that might be just what you want for your child, or you may walk away with some new additions to your bank of information and broaden your resources.

Getting Started

Now that you know what the job entails and how to go about it or how to get started, you must be prepared for the next step. These networking skills will help facilitate the advocacy process in moving one step closer to attaining the sought goals for your special needs child (advocacy is covered in Chapter 4).

Before we approach the topic of networking, there is one factor that's important to keep in mind throughout this whole process. While networking might be quite new to you and can feel threatening and overwhelming, it can also be a wonderful process. Don't be afraid to call people you have never met who are referred to you by friends. Usually these are parents of children with special needs, who are more than happy to assist and share information. For some of us, this may be a very difficult step to take. We are very private and are used to solving problems on our own. Requesting assistance does not come easily—we feel as if we are imposing on others. We are good at volunteering or helping others out, but when it comes time for us to reach out and ask for help, we recoil.

Though this may be a difficult step for us to take, it is important that we make changes in our way of thinking. As we have stated before, finding information or services can at times be elusive, and remaining in isolation can have negative results. You have a lot to gain by reaching out.

When you first call, introduce yourself and explain how you got the person's name. Give a very short explanation of why you are calling, and ask for a good time for you to call or meet. This provides the person you are calling the opportunity to talk with you at a time that is mutually convenient. At times, these phone calls can lead to important connections and friendships. You never know where a phone call could lead, so never shortchange yourself by not following a lead or suggestion, no matter how inconsequential it may seem. And on the other side of the coin, you could be helping, by being a resource for the person you are calling. How wonderful to be an advocate for your child and simultaneously helping someone else out. Granted, there will be telephone calls to people who won't be receptive or who will be frustrating to deal with, but there will also be telephone calls or correspondence with people who turn out to be so much more than anticipated.

Sandy: So many times, I've gotten on the telephone and stated my needs, only to find out that the person knows me from somewhere in the past, or is a neighbor that I didn't know, or has a personal story to share that can lead to some other resource not originally being sought. The unexpected results can be rewarding and quite fun. They can also be another source of support. While we are seeking support services or resources, we might come across people along the way who listen to our needs and are very supportive and offer information never anticipated. The bottom line is not to look at this process as a negative procedure but rather as something uplifting, hopeful, and promising, to move your child ahead in the world.

Maria: I remember the time I joined Special Connection, a support and resource group for parents of children with special needs. On several occasions, I was told to call a woman in my neighborhood who had a child with special needs similar to my child's and who was going through the same school system and could provide me with useful information based on her experience. I hesitated calling, afraid I would be intruding, and then easily forgot about it as I concentrated on dealing with my own day-to-day issues. When her name came up again at another meeting, I made the resolution to call that same evening and stop wasting time. This woman and I had to reschedule several times before we were able to meet, but when we finally met, we found so much to talk about and share that I truly regretted not calling her earlier. I made a new friend, found someone who clearly understood what I was talking about, and walked away with some wonderful advice. Once again, my sense of isolation was replaced by the knowledge that I was not alone and did not need to remain alone.

Just remember, sympathy from friends is valuable support; empathy is the ultimate support.

Networking Activities

Let us now take a more in-depth look at those networking activities that are available. Each one by itself can prove to be tremendously helpful, but in combination, all of these sources can be the major key to empowering you as a parent. How you access any of the sources available basically follows the same format, whether it is an organization or a summer or educational program.

One must have a mastery of the tools to implement this process. Whether you're using the telephone book or a reference book, or you're merely speaking up and asking, these tools can all be applied to getting what you want or need. The old adage "Try, try again" can certainly be applied here. If the first source you seek doesn't materialize into what you are looking for, move on. Don't get stuck, and most of all, don't get frustrated. Don't leave any stone unturned. Remember rule number three: follow every lead, no matter how inconsequential. You might ask a teacher, for instance, if there are any support groups for parents, and the teacher may lead you to a group that you don't feel quite comfortable with. Move on from there, by asking someone else where you can find a support group. In another case, the teacher might not know of a support group but can put you in touch with a parent or another professional who does know of a support group. Write down every source and keep it organized in the folders for future use, but don't throw anything out and don't give up. We can't emphasize this enough nor repeat it enough.

One of the logical places to start gathering information is from the organizations that provide services and information to support the special needs community. A simple place to start locating the various organizations is the school or the hospital that is servicing or has serviced your child in the past. Often, school personnel—the classroom teacher, the school psychologist, or the principal—can provide the information you are seeking. And if they don't know of any organizations, they might be able to put you in touch with others who do know. Doctors, nurses, and social services can also be an excellent source. Open yourself up to the world around you and make contacts. Community and religious leaders, family members, and neighbors can all be wonderful sources leading you to the organizations that provide the services you need. These people can even put you in touch with other parents. Thus, you can see how the wheels of networking are starting to turn.

When seeking organizations, you might not need their services immediately, but it's a good idea to keep a record of who they are and what they do. Even if you call an organization and you feel over the telephone that it is probably not appropriate, ask to have a brochure sent anyway. This should be done for several reasons. The brochure might list other organizations, individuals, or other services that they offer, which perhaps you weren't aware of in your telephone conversation. You can access other pieces of information that you didn't even realize you were looking for. If the brochure has nothing to do with anything you need, and the organization or program does not meet your needs at the time, pass the brochure on to someone you feel it may help. Bring it to a support group, for instance, and mention it to others. Before you do this, however, jot down in your records the name of the organization, its address and telephone number, and what the organization does. Then, in the future, if you ever do need the services of this organization, you will already have its name and telephone number. Sometimes, an organization will ask if you want to be on its mailing list for future programs or brochures. Don't overlook this, either, because the organization might change in structure and expand in their services, and you will want to be kept abreast of what is happening.

When calling an organization for a brochure, make a note in your records of the fact that you did call, when you did, and when you can expect the brochure. Sometimes an organization will take your name and address and tell you its new brochure won't be out for a few weeks or months and that they will send it to you at a later date. With our hectic lives, this is one thing we don't need to remember—just write it down, and then if the brochure doesn't come when anticipated, you can call back.

Although organizations are invaluable, your connection with other special needs parents is indispensable. The organization might give you the newsletter, the resources, the conferences, keeping you up to date on the latest in special needs. Yet it is the parent who helps you extract what will be most tailored for you. Sharing and comparing notes is the foundation for building the bridges that connect first the parents to the world and then their child. Other parents often provide information and resources relevant to the community you live in or in those communities close by with programs or services accessible to you. They provide you with information as well as identifiable emotions.

This communication with other parents of children with special needs also serves as a way of establishing important connections within the community, essential to your emotional well-being and sense of belonging, to your need to have peers with whom you can share similar interests and concerns, and with whom you can create a presence and a voice within your community.

Although there is a common thread in the use of networking to fulfill your needs, there are slight variations in the manner in which you proceed. For instance, in seeking a doctor for your child, your references might come from the pediatrician, or they might come from another parent. It seems that the special needs parent can be the ultimate source for so many avenues. After all, if they have experienced it firsthand, that can be better than someone who just knows the name of a contact.

Don't be afraid to test new waters. But always keep in mind that different people experience sources in different ways. Asking for suggestions means looking and exploring alternatives. As you explore leads, your opinions about some of them may differ from those who made the suggestion. You should not be afraid to have different opinions no matter how well others have done with that specialist, service, or program. Think of the advice as a springboard to launch you into other areas, if they are more appropriate. Just because a doctor might be the "absolute greatest" for this parent's child does not necessarily mean that he or she will be the one for your child. Each child is different, and the personalities may not gel or a child may not feel comfortable with one particular sex. One child may prefer the loud, booming voice of a doctor, while another child's needs may call for a softer, slower manner. You need to be aware of your child's needs and strike a happy balance between the doctor's professional capabilities and the chemistry that will work best with your child. A doctor may have the utmost professional credentials and experience, yet if your child does not feel at ease with this doctor and has a difficult time with each impending visit, causing great anxiety to the child, then you may want to rethink the situation and perhaps consider a different selection.

As stated earlier, none of these sources are mutually exclusive, nor are the tools to find them. The same mouth that you opened up to ask for an organization is the same one that can secure the right doctor or the right educational, recreational, or summer program.

Speaking up also involves the telephone. What a wonderful means of accessing information! From one spot, you can reach out to so many avenues. The telephone networking source has its own personal list of our do's and don'ts. Although many of these suggestions may seem quite obvious and basic, it does not hurt to review them and thus sharpen your awareness of these very helpful steps. To start with, never make a phone call without paper and pencil in front of you. And when jotting down an additional number, always identify it. How many times have we made a phone call, written the suggested number, perhaps another number next to it, then later couldn't figure out what that number referred to. By not identifying that number, you have complicated the process and made more work for yourself. Counterproductive! Always write down the person to whom you are speaking and especially their extension. With the new world of telephone menus, having the extension immediately on hand can save you from listening to everything the "telephone restaurant" has to offer. As you write down all of this information, make sure you do so in a legible manner. How often have we looked at our scribbles to find out that we can't read the number or the name we have written, rendering the information useless or forcing us to retrace our steps and retrieve the original source?

When you are given a possible lead with a phone number, do not give up if the first call you make doesn't provide all the information you want. Often you may need to call several numbers, just to be told to call another number because the number you've called is not the right person/department or source for the information you need. Be persistent—it usually pays off—and in the process, you sometimes come across new sources of information. In time, you also become better at asking more precisely and accurately for information by using some of the lingo typical in the field.

One important tip when embarking on a possible telephone runaround is to plan to do such phone calls at a time when it is quiet and you have time to calmly make one phone call after the other without getting angry at the person on the other end of the line.

Don't try to fit some of these calls in when you are in a rush to go somewhere and have limited time to pursue the leads or different departments within an organization.

Another hint: When you are talking to one extension and they offer to transfer you to another, request the number of that extension before being transferred, so that if you get disconnected you can call back directly. You always want to be in the driver's seat, even on the telephone. If you leave a message on voice mail and you have the option to hear it back, do so. Make sure you didn't forget any important information, especially your telephone number. As you are forwarded from one extension to the other, someone along the line may suggest transferring you to a number you have already spoken to. Speak up and say you have already tried that extension/source and ask what else they can suggest. At times, you do reach dead ends, but in many situations, you sooner or later come across what you are looking for.

If you are leaving the message with a real live person, get that person's name, in case there is a miscommunication. *Never hang up without getting the person's name.* Having the person's name is an invaluable piece of information. It's much easier to make return calls and refer to a certain individual by name than to say that you spoke to someone but you cannot provide any information as to who that someone may be. When there is a problem or misunderstanding, it is much easier to resolve it when you can provide the names of the people you have spoken to—they may be able to clarify the situation more expediently if you can access them rather than start from scratch. Also, if you are told that the particular person is not there when you call back, tell whoever answers what your situation is all about and see if this person can help you. *Get that person's name.* Be a secretary, be active, be on top of it.

A further tip is to ask if there is a direct line to that extension so you can avoid the menu altogether and go right to the dessert. This is especially helpful when the company and the switchboard may be closed, but the person you are seeking is still working. Writing down the date and time you left a message is also essential, so that you can judge the appropriate time to wait before calling back if you don't receive a return phone call in a suitable amount of time. And just what is suitable? That is a hard question to answer. It depends on the nature of the problem. That will have to be left up to your best judgment. But don't be afraid to call a number again even if you have been told that they will get back to you. In this fast-paced world, even with the best of intentions, people can get caught up in their own pace and forget to return a call. At least ask for a time frame in which that return call may occur. And speaking of afraid, don't be telephone-shy. You are only doing what is best for your child. If you come across a difficult person, don't be afraid to ask for someone else to assist you.

Another factor to consider is the person you are calling. For instance, you might be given a lead on a person to contact about a certain organization. You call that person and find that you are constantly leaving messages. The best thing to do is get to an operator, especially if there are many electronic menus, and ask if there is someone else who can help you. Often, several people can help you but just one name was thrown out to you. If the original name that you were given turns out to be the only person who can help you and you are having a hard time reaching this person or end up playing telephone tag, tell someone else in the organization about your dilemma, and perhaps they can reach the person you are seeking. If you just need an answer to a question, then leave a message for that person to leave the information on your answering machine.

When you do reach a dead end, it may be due to the fact that what you are looking for is not currently available. One question to ask yourself is, "Could it be available in another country?" Sometimes doctors, university professors, or special organizations may have information about programs or resources available in Canada or Europe, for example.

You may reach a dead end because you are barking up the wrong tree. "Who else can I ask? How else can I state what I need?"

Sometimes, phone calls may lead you nowhere. This is the time to share that deadlock with friends, doctors, etc. Someone may have a new name or have read something recently in a newspaper or magazine that may be just what you are looking for to put you back on track.

One last piece of advice. It is most disruptive to be talking to a source only to be interrupted by call-waiting. Unless you are waiting for a crucial telephone call, we highly recommend switching off call-waiting if you have that service on your telephone. And while we're on the topic of telephones, let's explore the telephone book. This too is a valuable source not to be overlooked. Sometimes you can just flip to the Yellow Pages and read it through, exploring different avenues. You can look up organizations; this in turn might refer you to another part of the phone book. You might discover an organization you didn't even know existed. It may have a vague connection to what you are looking for. Call it. Ask who they are and what they do. It may have nothing to do with your needs at all. But, remember, there are no dead ends in networking. All you've done is eliminated a source that isn't applicable. The "worst" that could happen is you discover a source you never even imagined or a source that could lead to one you need. Who knows, maybe the receptionist answering the phone is the sister of the brother of the uncle of the head of special needs in your state. Look up schools. There may be a school out there you have never heard of, but which might be referred to as a special school.

Many telephone books have a separate section for local, state, and federal agencies. Here, too, is an excellent place to look. You may not know what you are looking for, so just read it. They are not all that long. It's an amazing thing to do. You'll be amazed at how many services there are. Sometimes it helps to take a shot in the dark as a starting point. For example, if you are looking for information on advocacy, look in your telephone book for education under "Government Offices." Tell whoever answers what you are looking for and see if they can assist you in any way.

Maria: Last summer, I was asked by a friend to assist her in locating a camp that offered special education and English as a second language (ESL) programs. I started by calling a camp that offered ESL and a camp that offered special education. Both camps gave me names that eventually led to my locating two camps that offered this combination of services. It took a few telephone calls, but in the end, I was able to provide my friend with the information and services that she needed for her child.

Other sources of information are parent newspapers or your local newspaper. They are good sources of information on camps, upcoming community events, stores with educational toys, etc.

Networking does require one possibly difficult task of you, the parent. In order to get to where you want to go, you have to open your mouth. This means exposing to the world your private story, at times also sharing your private sorrow. In order to access what you need, you have to say what you need, and this can be more difficult for some parents than others.

Sandy: I often compare it to a fillet of fish. I feel like I have been opened up. Sometimes I don't want to tell one more person my nightmare, my anguish, but in the end I know that this is what will be best for my child.

An organization, person, camp, school, or whatever source you are endeavoring to network with cannot help you or your child if they don't know what your needs are. It's important not to downgrade these feelings or their difficulties, but to put these aside in the best interests of the child. Say what you need, and in turn get what you need. If you follow this credo, it might be less difficult emotionally. It can be a difficult transition from the private world to the public world. This credo can help smooth out that transition. It is the nature of the process, and just that. This is what will ultimately be the best means for getting the job done and moving your child ahead in the world.

Another way to look at it, which might also help in this transition, is to consider the role model you are providing. Parents set the precedent for their children to fend for themselves when they're on their own. You are setting the values and teaching your child how to cope in this world. The letting-go process of parent and child is difficult as it is, but even more so if your child has special needs. The more your child can adopt the networking tools that you have so skill-fully used, the better equipped the child will be to advance in this world. So, this is another road we are endeavoring to pave for our children. Not just making the path smooth, but teaching our children how to continue on this path of networking and to be as skillful as possible at it. Ernest Hemingway put it so well when he said, "Catch a fish and you eat for a day, teach someone to fish and they eat for a lifetime."

Welcome to the world of networking!

4

Advocacy

Advocacy is defined as "providing support," and an advocate is
one "who pleads the cause of another."

While networking is the search and exchange of ideas
and resources, advocacy is the direct involvement in active
negotiation on your child's behalf, and the ongoing supervision of your child's programs, services, healthcare, and
schoolwork. You are the crucial intermediary between your
child and the outside world.

Advocating on behalf of a child with special needs is
important, because although people may agree that these
children have a right to free and appropriate education,
they tend to disagree on what that means. Social, political,
and economic factors greatly influence what services, educational programs, adaptive equipment, transportation, etc.
that these children will receive (James E. Ysseldyke and Bob
Algozzine, *Introduction to Special Education, 2nd ed.,*
Houghton Miflin Company, Boston, 1990).

The changes brought about in the education services and in the legal protection of children with special needs is largely the result of the work of parents, advocacy groups, and professionals committed to assisting children/people with special needs to achieve their rights (Ysseldyke and Algozzine, 1990).

There are formal advocacy groups, for example, the National Association for Retarded Citizens (NARC) and the Learning Disabilities Association (LDA). These groups have ensured individuals with special needs their rights by focusing their efforts on state and federal legislation. Advocacy groups have also taken action in pressuring colleges, universities, and other advanced professional schools to provide programs that will meet the needs of exceptional students (Ysseldyke and Algozzine, 1990).

On the home front, as parents we need to become advocates for our children by becoming actively involved in the process of special education. We need to become and to feel empowered to request services we deem necessary, to raise questions or concerns (about our children's educational program, evaluation, etc.), to disagree with professionals when necessary, to seek second opinions, to expect and demand respect for our views, and to be actively included in the decision-making process affecting our children's development and education.

There is now more of an expectation for parents to have an active role in their children's care and educational needs. Studies have indicated that children do better in school when parents show interest and support in their education. This is particularly true of special education. The more parents understand the process of special education and their rights under the law, the better prepared they will be to ensure that their children receive the appropriate support and services assured by laws and legislation.

Parents no longer should receive advice from professionals in a passive manner. They should receive information from many different sources and make their own decisions about what is best for their child (Kirk, Gallagher, and Anastasiow, 1993).

Since we have defined what advocacy is, let's explore its many components. For many parents (speaking from experience), becoming active participants in the special education process can be very intimidating and frightening. "Where do I start?" "What am I supposed to do?" "What if my questions are stupid?" "Is what I am asking for inappropriate?" These are just a few of the common and important questions that will pop into your mind.

Faced with the realization that your child has special needs, you may respond in different ways. Some parents immediately throw themselves into the process with unbelievable energy and drive. Some may go through a process of denial and refuse to take action or drag their feet through every step they need to take. Others will start slowly, frightened by the lack of guidance and their lack of knowledge of a world they never dreamed they would be part of. These are normal and typical responses. For those who may initially have difficulty starting or who move cautiously at first, support groups and parent organizations can provide you with the information and support you need to embark on a long and at times difficult journey.

Parental participation or advocacy is facilitated by accessing support, by acquiring knowledge, and by understanding that this process is going to take time and be ongoing. At times, information will be readily available; at other times, you might feel as if the information you need is elusive.

The following tips/suggestions may assist you in getting started in your role as advocate for your child:

1. Familiarize yourself with as much information regarding your child's condition/needs/issues/disorder/disability by:

- Reading relevant books, journals, articles, or viewing educational videos. You can access some of this material by checking the education section at bookstores, by asking your doctors, therapists, and teachers for suggested readings, and by calling the Department of Special Education in local colleges or universities.
- Talking to other parents, particularly parents with special needs children (see Chapter 3, "Networking").

2. Familiarize yourself with your legal rights. You can get some of this information by calling your state Department of Education, Office of Special Education and requesting a copy of the federal regulations governing the education of a child with special needs and copies of any available literature written for parents.

3. Prepare a file, box, or drawer where you can keep important, relevant information (see Chapter 2, "Getting Organized"). If you find a good article or video that might assist others (teachers, relatives, siblings, etc.) in understanding your child, share it with them when possible. The more information you share with others, the better educated our society will become regarding children with special needs.

Maria: I have made many copies of articles, which I have shared with my daughter's teachers. I have also shared these articles with other parents, friends, and relatives in need of information for themselves or for a friend. I am constantly on the lookout for all sorts of articles that may be of interest to me or to friends. I am always saving and sharing information.

By sharing information and educating others about various special needs, we help to dispel erroneous notions about our children's needs, behavior, potential, etc. The lack of knowledge and understanding of others is one of our main sources of frustration and aggravation. People often offer well-meaning advice and suggestions on how to discipline or raise our children without realizing that what we are doing is based on educationally sound guidelines and goals set by our child's therapist, doctor, counselor, or IEP team.

Maria: One video I have shared with my children, husband, friends, and colleagues is *FAT City Workshop* by Richard Lavoie (FAT stands for fear, anxiety, and tension), which helps parents, siblings, and teachers experience and understand the world of a child with learning disabilities (LD). It provides viewers with an opportunity to experience the frustrations of children with LD and to reflect on the typical reactions these children encounter when they fail to meet the expectations of others. It is a film that gives you understanding and food for thought.

4. Contact the special education office in your school district and inquire about programs, locations, and personnel. If you are relocating to a new community or state, this is a very important step to take. Special education programs vary considerably in their scope and quality across communities and states as a reflection of social, political, or economic variances.

5. Contact your local Parent Advisory Council (PAC). You should be able to get this information by calling the special education office in your school district. These groups meet on a regular (monthly) basis to discuss parents' concerns with the special education programs, to invite speakers in the field, and to provide parents with an opportunity to meet other parents in the school districts, keeping them abreast of changes, issues, and other relevant information.

6. Join a local parent support group. If one is not available, consider starting one.

7. Join a state or national organization that might provide you with newsletters, information on upcoming conferences, workshops, presentations, resources, and updates on legislature or changes in laws affecting the special needs population.

8. If you are attending a school meeting (initial IEP meeting, reevaluation, or review), consider inviting the therapist or physician who works with your child outside the school, who might provide important information and/or insight on your child. If scheduling does not permit these professionals to attend the meetings, consider scheduling a meeting with them and asking, from their perspective, what they would like you to share or discuss about your child or what information they would like to receive from the school.

9. Consider having someone you feel comfortable with and trust attend the school meeting with you. This person could be a spouse, friend, teacher, professional advocate, or perhaps another parent with a special needs child. It has to be someone who will respect your child's privacy, since in some cases very specific, personal, and confidential information will be discussed.

These meetings can sometimes feel very intimidating or be tense. Having someone there with you can be helpful in a variety of ways:

During the meeting, the other person can:

- Take notes
- Help you clarify issues raised
- Help you restate your points or requests if you are not being understood
- Give you confidence

After the meeting, the other person can:

- Discuss and share observations about the meeting
- Help you clarify or reconfirm any concerns or reassurances stated during the meeting
- Assist you in strategizing how to pursue an issue that is causing friction between your family and the school team (more on IEP meetings in Chapter 6)

10. Contact your child's teacher early in the school year and frequently touch base in an informal manner. Ask how things are going and if there is anything that you can do to assist your child at home. It is important to have an idea of how your child is adjusting academically, socially, and emotionally during the year, for the following reasons:

- To see if the IEP goals are being addressed and what progress is being made.
- To be aware of new issues that might emerge, which you might want to include/add to your child's IEP, or to explore what other programs, resources, or support is available in your school system for your child that you may need to access at this time.

11. You may also want to consider out-of-school resources that might assist your child and alleviate some of the difficulties your child may be experiencing before the problem or difficulty becomes more serious or problematic. This could involve an academic tutor, a peer therapy group, lessons, etc.

Advocacy incorporates staying on top of a situation once you have settled into it. After you have spoken up or done your research to find the "perfect program," you have to be aware of how that program is progressing. Just because you think you have found the perfect program, based on research, referrals, or whatever, there is no guarantee that it is the right program. You need to observe and ask questions of the facilitator and your child as well to make sure that this is really working. Asking open-ended questions is always important in dialogues, but here is a case in which it especially applies.

Let's take the example of a special art program that you have found for your child. Through networking and advocacy tactics, you are told this is a wonderful program to help your child with eye-hand coordination. It's important that you know who the teacher is, if possible try to observe the class, and when asking your child about the program, ask in a way that you will know just what is going on. "How was art today?" might only produce an answer of "good." But questions such as "What did you paint today?" or "What did the teacher say about your project?" or "Did you enjoy doing that particular type of art?" are going to get you much better answers with more information. Take cues from your child as well. If your child starts protesting about going or doesn't seem enthusiastic, perhaps you need to look into it. It might be something about the teacher, another child in the class, or just that this may

not be the appropriate situation for your child. It may be
something easily identifiable and easily corrected, or it may
go deeper. The bottom line is to be aware of the situation,
take the cues, and follow through on them.

Sandy: Something happened to my daughter that made
me realize how very important it is to be "on top of it all."
My daughter Rayna loves to sing, and I started networking
to find her a singing teacher. My path took me to a local
singing teacher from a school, who also taught privately at
home. Rayna started her lessons, and as the weeks went on,
I began to sense that something wasn't quite right. Rayna
didn't have the enthusiasm that she usually has about
singing and didn't seem to look forward to her lessons. I
started listening to the lessons and tried to figure out just
what was wrong. I began to sense that there wasn't a chemistry between Rayna and the teacher, and I began to realize
that the teacher didn't have a sense about dealing with
Rayna. I was beginning to pinpoint the problem and was
trying to decide what to do about it and how much more
time to wait before taking some action, when the teacher
made a comment to me that started me investigating in
another direction.

Because of Rayna's medical condition, every time she
begins any new program, I give the teacher a brief synopsis
of her problem, using the simplest terms that will convey
the information as succinctly as possible. I usually summarize it by saying that Rayna had a bleed in her brain, like a
stroke, when she was three and has right-sided weaknesses
as a result. Anything further than that is usually discussed
if the teacher or facilitator isn't sure how to proceed. On
this particular lesson, only about the fifth or sixth week,
the teacher approached me and told me that Rayna was

complaining of dizziness when she was singing and that the teacher was concerned because of her medical condition. Because I am the mother of a child with a medical condition, I immediately began to panic that something was wrong with my child and because of her medical condition she wouldn't even be able to sing, which was something she truly enjoyed. So many other areas were difficult for her, so many other doors were closed or hard to open— why singing too? Totally distraught, I decided to go for that good old second opinion, and once again mustered up the energy to start the networking procedure all over again.

I found another singing teacher approximately half an hour away. I called her, repeated the entire story to her, and she said she would do an evaluation of Rayna. The day I was supposed to take her, I found myself quite anxious, not wanting to believe that something Rayna truly enjoys could also be cut off from her. The teacher turned out to be a warm, caring person, very bubbly. She listened to Rayna, having her sing scales at all different levels, doing a variety of vocal exercises, and pinpointing when Rayna got dizzy. She turned to the both of us after the lesson and informed me that Rayna had a beautiful voice with lots of potential. The dizziness occurred when she hit certain high notes, because her vocal chords weren't used to it and she didn't know how to breathe properly; with a few lessons in proper breathing for singing, the dizziness should disappear. She, in fact, had seen this situation many times in new singers and it always disappeared with proper training. I was so relieved at this news.

Rayna started taking lessons from the second teacher. Sure enough, within three or four lessons, Rayna stopped complaining of the dizziness. There were so many life lessons to be learned from this. I knew that I never again would let myself get in this kind of situation, that I would always be right on top of what is happening, and that I would try not to panic until I got all the facts, which in many cases might mean seeking out different sources. Rayna still takes lessons to this day and has never once complained of dizziness in the last three years since starting with the new teacher. My favorite question I get from people when I tell them I drive half an hour for her lesson is, "You drive all the way there for singing lessons?" And my favorite answer is "Yes!" This teacher is a wonderful source for Rayna and a caring, devoted person. Perhaps I could start the networking search again to find someone closer, but we are all happy and content with this teacher, so why change?

It takes a lot of emotional energy to network, even more to advocate, and even more to sustain, change, or move on. But it's all important and worth it in the end if the teacher and the program are right for your child. It's very important not to let yourself get locked into a situation, to realize that this teacher and/or the program are not necessarily the only path to follow, and if it isn't working out, it may be time to move on and start the search again. There is a fine line between knowing that a particular program or teacher isn't right and giving something a chance to work out. We don't have any magic formula on this. Take your cues and listen to them carefully. Listen to what your child is saying and follow through on anything that doesn't seem quite right.

Sandy: Instead of discovering that my child's medical condition was impeding on an artistic talent she wanted to develop, I simply discovered that this teacher wasn't the proper one for my child.

In simple terms, advocacy is standing up for your child and fighting on his or her behalf. It is keeping your eyes and ears open for new avenues to explore or to put a stop to situations that are counterproductive. At times, it can energize you and propel you to attain what initially seemed difficult or complex. It can also be draining, because it is an ongoing process. It is important, though, to remember that life in general requires us to advocate for ourselves and for our children. Our children's special needs may force us to sharpen these skills and become more adept at them. But all of our children require our support in negotiating the outside world.

Advocacy is inherent in being a parent in this world. We all want what is best for our children, to have them live in a world that brings them only the best. Everyday life is synonymous with advocating. Each skill we teach and each new step along the way is a means to an end, a means to be advocating for the children. What we have endeavored to do in this chapter is break down the various skills that are necessary not just for any child, but for the special needs child. There are crossovers and overlapping, because your special needs child is also your child. The same advocating you do for the nonspecial needs child is also done for the special needs child, it's just tailor-made for each child. Some advocating may be the same and some may be very different, or some may be the same with two branches, one for each type of child. In any case, the bottom line is the thread of advocacy that follows one through life, helps one get what is wanted, where it's wanted, and successfully.

5

The Special Needs Child in the Medical World

There are some special needs children for whom learning disabilities is the main or only part of their special needs, but there are many children whose daily lives are caught up in medical problems as well. Some of these children will only have medical problems, while others will have both medical and learning special needs. In this chapter we will address the issue of the special needs child in the medical world so that you, the parent, can better help your child.

Many hours might be spent in a doctor's office and/or in hospitals, and this can add much stress to you, your child, and the entire family. Your routines and lifestyle expectations might be drastically affected. Whether dealing with a one-time visit, a many-time occurrence, or a hospitalization, there are many strategies that can help smooth the way. First, let's take a look at the doctor's visits, and then we can address hospitalization.

Before the Appointment

You've just been told to take your child to a doctor. Something needs further investigating; something suggests that perhaps a specialist is needed. Your safe world is no longer safe. You are scared and apprehensive. You've been given this information by another doctor, a teacher, or a therapist. The bottom line is, you need to visit a doctor. Whether it is a mild problem or a serious problem, the fact that you need to step into the sterile world of medicine for something other than the routine physical, earaches, or stomach bugs causes you to worry. The first onset of anxiety finds its source in the unknown. "What is wrong with my child?" Worst-case scenarios creep into your imagination even when you're not aware of it. We refer to this time as the "waiting game." You're waiting for the appointment, and until that appointment happens, your life hangs in a precarious balance, an unsettled state.

"Do I enroll my child in the ballet class? What if the doctor says. . . ?"

"Will Billy still be able to go on the camping trip? What if the doctor says. . . ?"

"What about school, what about the Saturday dance, what about. . . ?"

"What if the doctor tells me this or that or THIS and THAT. . . ?"

The best thing you can do for yourself is to behave normally, sticking to the family routines. This gives not only you a sense of security and stability but your child and any other members of the family as well. If everyone in the family can stick to the daily routines as closely as possible, then this medical interruption might not be as overwhelming. There is a sense of security when familiarity and rituals don't get drastically altered. Although this isn't always totally possible, it is a goal to aim for as much as can possibly be achieved. Avoid situations such as whispering on the telephone about it whenever someone calls. Children are incredibly perceptive and can pick up on moods, changes in the ambience of the household, and deviant behavior patterns. If you usually chitchat on the kitchen phone, but lately you've been telling your caller to hold on and then move to a closed room, your child can become alarmed, especially if the child is aware of the impending doctor's appointment.

We firmly believe in letting your child know what is going on, to be as honest as possible, but at the appropriate level, using age-appropriate language. News delivered to a three-year-old is clearly given in a different fashion than to an eighteen-year-old. The substance of the information should be the same: clear, honest facts about what is going on so that the child will understand why he has to go to the doctor. Then he won't have sleepless nights. One or two adults in the household doing that is more than enough!

> "Susie, honey, the teacher thinks you might be having a little problem understanding what the teacher is saying, especially when she reads you a story at story hour, so we're going to a special doctor who will help tell us why, so we can try to make it easier for you in school."
>
> "Bill, the teacher is concerned about you falling asleep in class, and finals are coming up. She suggested that we visit Dr. Martin, so we'll be going on Thursday. You know, check out mono or the possibility of a virus."

This also includes other family members, such as siblings. It's important for them to know what is going as as well. A sibling can be very frightened when something of this magnitude is happening in the family. Depending on the nature of the special need and the age of the sibling, different tactics need to be used.

Sandy: When my daughter Rayna was diagnosed, her older sister, Tovah, was only five. The pediatrician appeared at our house the night of the diagnosis and talked at length to everyone in the family. He advised us to make it very clear to the older sibling that she didn't cause what happened to Rayna and also that what Rayna had was nothing that her sister could also get. These were the two key messages for us to convey to our five-year-old.

The term we use for siblings of special needs children is *special siblings*. These special siblings are also affected by any changes in the household concerning the special needs child. The special needs child may be the one who is going to the appointment or being hospitalized, but everyone is affected by a "difference" in the household. The following tips can help create a calmer atmosphere when tending to the needs of the special sibling. Once again, each situation varies. We realize that these are the optimum goals, and they can't always be planned or fulfilled. However, they are general considerations to keep in mind.

Make sure the siblings are cared for in a way that you, as well as the siblings, feel comfortable with. Ask yourself if the children will be happier staying with a favorite relative, friend, or baby-sitter; if at all possible, try to leave the children where they would like to be. Ask the siblings what they would like or would feel more comfortable with. This will make the siblings feel more empowered in this upsetting situation.

Make arrangements so that their schedules and activities aren't interrupted.

Make sure you give yourself what we call *appointment space*, i.e., don't tighten your schedule so that you are in a hurry to return from the appointment to get Susie to a ballet class. Arrange for the sitter or a car pool to be on hand to take Susie wherever she needs to go, so that if you are at the appointment unexpectedly longer than anticipated, no one is under stress or is disappointed.

If you are running late, call home. Let the caretaker know what is going on. Depending on the age or maturity of the child, direct conversation will either be appropriate or not. A young sibling who is feeling settled and comfortable with the caretaker might be upset by the sound of your voice, and in that case, the caretaker needs to be the one to relay the message. In other cases, talking directly to the sibling might be the right thing to do.

In some cases, it might be appropriate for the sibling to go with you, to see what is going on, whether waiting in the waiting room with a secretary or actually sitting in on the appointment.

Sandy: I remember after Rayna was in physical therapy for years, my older daughter asked me one day if she could come to one of her appointments. I spoke to the therapist and arranged the visit. It was wonderful. Rayna's sister got to see just what Rayna does in physical therapy. Another time, when Rayna was hospitalized, both Rayna and her sister went to the playroom and made some art projects with the play therapist. They had equal dosages of fun and distraction. Two beautiful glitter paintings were proudly taken home in the suitcase. When we returned home, I saw that I hadn't packed them properly, and I now had a shining lining to the suitcase. I smiled. Happy memories amidst unhappy circumstances.

Before the appointment, it may also be a good idea to call ahead for directions, parking availability, and to inquire whether the doctor is running on time. Also, ask what floor and room number the office is located at, so that you don't have to take time to find a directory or an information desk. This is especially helpful if you do run late. Leave yourself plenty of time to get there, in case of traffic or getting lost. Try not to have other things scheduled after the appointment that you may feel stress getting back to. Besides taking care of the sibling's activities, your own calendar should be freed up as much as possible. This isn't always possible, but the less "external" anxiety to the appointment, the less stressed you will be.

There are three kinds of doctor's appointments: one that the child actually goes on, one that just the parents attend, and one in which the child is in the room and the doctor asks the child to leave so he can talk to the parents alone.

Sandy: Yes, it's important to obtain information from the doctor that shouldn't be heard in front of the child; yet the mere fact that the child is being asked to leave the room may conjure up the fear of "What is it that they don't want me to know?" After all these years, I still don't have a magic answer to this one. There are no set rules and no givens. What works in some situations doesn't necessarily work in every situation. My best advice in this area, like in so many other ambiguous areas, is to go with your best instincts. Perhaps the best concrete answer I could offer would be to call ahead and ask the doctor if he prefers to speak to the parents alone, and then prepare the child in advance.

> "Bill, I heard that Dr. Smith will want to talk with all (or both) of us, then he'll review everything with the parents alone. Why don't you bring the history homework with you so you can work on it in the waiting room?"
>
> "Susie, honey, sometimes the doctor likes to talk to the grown-ups alone. I'll bring some crayons so you can color while you wait."

Being prepared is much better than being surprised. This leads us into another area of the appointment. Often, we have taken our child for a visit and were taken right on time. But, just as often, we have had to wait because the doctor was running late or had an unexpected emergency. Time can be spent most efficiently if you're prepared in advance. When bringing a small child, bring books to read, coloring, or any other applicable activities to help pass the time, especially ones that will bring the most comfort to the child. Bring something for you, as well, so that if the child is playing independently, you can catch up on your reading or work. You might be the kind of person to just sit and think and people-watch, or you may want to bring your writing or a book just in case. It is also good to have busy work for your child in case unexpected time is going to be spent waiting.

Sandy: On more than one occasion, we would see the neurologist and he would suggest a certain test, and the hospital would be able to fit us in that day. Sometimes we would go immediately, other times they would schedule it in an hour or so. What sometimes started out as a short appointment would end up being a whole day at the hospital. We learned to bring snacks and juices. Although hospital cafeterias offer healthy foods, we always found it better to have some things with us as well. Sometimes the cafeteria would be a bit of a walk and we wouldn't have that much time, or it would be right at the busiest hour. Being armed with some food and drink always helped. Also, if your child has a favorite animal, doll, or blanket, bring it. This is especially helpful if an unexpected test is ordered and your child will feel more comfortable with a sense of home. I would throw things into a tote bag, especially in the winter, when I would be carrying jackets, hats, toys, and food. These are just some of the fine-tuning ideas that can help make a visit to a doctor or hospital appointment smoother and less stressful.

Do not leave for the doctor's appointment without a smile and the notebook. That's right, the notebook.

From the moment you found out that you needed to take your child to a specialist, questions were exploding in your head and anxieties were rising. You started thinking of things that you hadn't thought of earlier. You started thinking of questions and concerns. The best way to channel all this is to write it down. No matter how simple or complex the question, write it down. Keep a notebook on you at all times. Think of it as your grocery list, shopping for answers and information to help your child. Relying on your memory is not productive in this case, because nerves are frayed, you might be overtired, your child might need extra attention, all making it difficult for you to focus on yourself. Also, information and language is new, making it difficult to understand, thus making it difficult to remember clearly.

Sandy: A second notebook that we found ourselves using when Rayna was diagnosed was a minitelephone book. Due to the rare nature of Rayna's illness, we felt the need to seek different opinions. A myriad of names, addresses, and telephone numbers were coming our way, some of which we didn't need immediately but were long-term suggestions to call on later. We started keeping all the telephone numbers in a little, yellow spiral notebook—our Yellow Pages of health and of hope. We even wrote down the secretary's name, the hours in which to call the doctor, which days the doctor was at which office and which hospital. One day, we went a little "crazy." We couldn't find the notebook. Rayna's hope for a cure existed in the little white lines of that book, and we couldn't find it. When we finally did, after much panic, yelling, and screaming, we immediately made a copy of the book, to keep at home in a safe place.

Remember to bring this notebook with you to the appointment. This way, you can write down any referrals or have a number readily available to give to the doctor. And if you do keep two copies of the notebook, remember to make the additions, deletions, or corrections that you make while on the appointment to the notebook at home, so that you can keep it up to date.

Okay, take your smile and your notebook, and you're off. Oh, and don't forget the child.

During the Appointment

Sleepless nights and agitated days become your lifestyle until the appointment, but alas, it's time to go to the doctor. It's time to find out what's wrong. Whether it's an ear check to start the investigation of why your child doesn't seem to understand the teacher, or a neurologist visit because there is concern of a serious condition, try not to show your anxiety. This will only make the doctor's visit more stressful for the child.

Sandy: I wish I had three ears. One to hear what the doctor says, one to let it go out the other ear in case I didn't like the news, and the third to let it back in, knowing it needs to be heard.

Sitting in the doctor's office can be an experience spanning a myriad of emotions. And most likely, no two doctor's appointments mirror themselves. But, you have your strength, all the courage you've been gathering since finding out about the appointment, and your notebook—use it! Remember to ask questions, no matter how inconsequential or simple they may seem. No question is too simple, especially when you are learning a whole new world filled with new vocabulary and new concepts. Don't ever be afraid to call with a question, whether in advance of the appointment, during it, or after. Don't let your fear of sounding uninformed prevent you from calling so that you can understand your child's situation better.

And write those answers down, and write them so you will understand them. A one-word answer at the time of the discussion might make perfect sense, but when digesting everything and rereading the notes, one-word notes might be confusing, ambiguous, and mostly, frustrating. But even if this happens with clear notes written, don't ever be afraid to call a doctor's office and ask for something to be explained again. After all, we are our children's best advocates, so advocate, whether medically, educationally, or otherwise.

Sandy: I know someone whose husband is in the medical field. Because of this, when they first started seeing a lot of doctors, she let him do all the talking and asking of questions. She soon realized this was a grave error. Later, she would ask him her questions. She would soak up the information from him and the doctor, yet she was taking a passive role during the appointment. She realized that this was ineffective. She needed to take more of a lead and ask her own questions. After that, whenever the doctor would ask for any questions, her notebook of questions would emerge, and she would ask her questions, write down answers, and be an actively integral part of the visit. Her questions were not necessarily ones that her husband would think of. As a mother, her outlook for her child comes from a different vantage point, and the issues that might pop in her head wouldn't necessarily pop in his. For instance, if she is the one who is the primary daily caretaker, then her daily interaction with her child might conjure up more domestic-oriented issues, such as bathing, sleeping, nutrition, personal grooming, etc.

Also, don't overlook the fact that the child may have some questions as well. The child may not feel comfortable asking the doctor directly, so after the appointment (see "After the Appointment") this can be addressed. Once again, depending on the age and other factors, the child may even have his or her own notebook and an agenda with the doctor.

After the Appointment

A doctor's appointment and/or hospital visit can be very unobtrusive, smooth, and a routine part of your daily schedule, not upsetting the harmony of the day. It can also be the most invasive attack on your emotions, carrying much stress, anxiety, and frustration. We've had our share of both kinds and many degrees in the middle. Although we advise in the earlier section "Before the Appointment" to do your best in freeing up a lot of time around the appointment, doing your best doesn't always necessarily add up to having the most ideal circumstances. You may not be able to free up the surrounding time to your best advantage, and you have to work within the confines of the time allotments. As we said, this can add additional stress. But even if you're in a hurry, there are some steps you should try to take immediately after the appointment.

As soon as possible after the visit, read over your notes, while they are fresh in your mind. You might discover something you thought you understood as you were writing it down, but now it doesn't make any sense, or you totally forgot to ask one of your questions. Don't hesitate to call the doctor back. You might not be able to talk to the doctor directly when you call, but tell the secretary (whose name you know!) why you are calling back and how they can reach you. This is where the advantage of having an answering machine can play an important role—we highly recommend one.

If what you forgot to ask the doctor is something like "Can Billy still play in the baseball game tonight?" tell the secretary what your question is. Don't just say you forgot to ask the doctor a question and ask to have a return call. The doctor may have left for surgery or an emergency and may not be able to get back to you until after the game is over. (If your question doesn't need immediate attention or is confidential, then wait for the doctor.) Ask the secretary to find out from the doctor what the answer is; you'll call back, or you can describe how you can be reached. How frustrating to have Billy miss the baseball game, only to find out it was perfectly okay for him to play. Doesn't Billy have enough problems without having to miss a baseball game that he could have played?

Discuss the appointment at the appropriate time and level with your child. For example, if the child was stressed during the appointment, review it with him. Find out what made it uncomfortable. Ask your child if he has any questions.

Sandy: Sometimes I found that there wasn't always an immediate reaction, but later in the day, my daughter would ask a question. Out of the blue she would ask something about the appointment or her medical status. People process information in different ways, and my best advice is to always be prepared for as much as you possibly can. Easier said than done!

If the doctor has ordered tests, talk about it. Unfortunately, we can't give you rules set in stone when it comes to so many of these areas. Sometimes it's better to wait until closer to the test time to discuss it, and sometimes it's better to discuss it immediately. Each situation has its own unique variables.

The doctor may suggest calling him back in a few weeks to let him know how your child is doing, or he may want a follow-up appointment in a year. Although many offices will send you reminder cards, it is a good idea to immediately write it down in your calendar or appointment book.

This is long-range information that doesn't require your immediate attention, but at the same time it must not be overlooked or forgotten. It is very easy to overlook or forget information down the road, so you need to have a way to remind yourself. You may want to write this in red pen or circle it, or write it across the top of the calendar. Use whatever method works to remind you to call back in a few days, weeks, months, or even a year. If you are told to make an annual appointment, you might want to write down a reminder on the calendar a few months in advance, not on the actual month that the appointment is required.

Another issue you must address involves seeking second opinions, and third, and fourth. . . . When to take the doctor's advice at face value and when to seek other opinions is not something totally clear. The old joke of a second opinion being great, as long as it agrees with the first, is certainly applicable here as well as in other areas. The more people you ask for opinions, both lay and professional, the more opportunities you open up for answers of a different nature. Sometimes these answers can be very similar, with just slight variations.

Sandy: In the case of Rayna, we had opinions that ran the gamut from leave it alone and watch it carefully to operate and to radiate. Even the school of thought that offered radiation differed among themselves in the kind of radiation. Talk about diverse! If you seek a second opinion and it agrees with the first, then some will think so be it. But there are others who might not feel satisfied until seeking several opinions. I found there is a fine line between looking for second opinions and looking for someone to tell me that there really isn't anything wrong with my child after all, despite CT scans, MRI results, etc. When I finally "accepted" that something was wrong with Rayna, I could separate this feeling from truly seeking other opinions as to what course of action to pursue next. Our second opinion, being so diverse in answers, made the final decision quite an ordeal, taking much research, investigation, and anxiety. We having the sinking feeling that no matter which opinion we followed, it would be the wrong choice. In the end, we chose the right one.

Life has no built-in guarantees, and this definitely applies to the category of medicine. Sometimes you need to take a risk when offered a treatment that is fairly new or experimental. You need to find out where the best place is and who the best person is to accomplish it. Sometimes the best place isn't necessarily in your own backyard. You might have to travel a distance in order to seek the appropriate treatment. The best way to approach this circumstance is to call ahead and obtain as much information as possible: where to stay, how to get there, insurance information, what you might need to bring, such as X rays and reports, and also long-term stay information, including special rates.

Sandy: Although I can't tell you what to do in each individual case, I can tell you to do your best not to leave any stone unturned. We turned every stone, and were lucky.

Before, during, or after an appointment—your lifestyle has changed. For some, this may be a singular experience. For others, it may be ongoing. Whatever the case, the bottom line is to be prepared and aware. It may not be humanly possible to control what is wrong with your child, but you can certainly be in the driver's seat for so many of the extraneous circumstances circumventing the situation. Helping to pave the way for the child, the special sibling, and all who are affected by this new circumstance will put you more in control. Being organized, prepared, and acquiring as much information as you can will help you better cope with the situation.

Here is our list of do's concerning the doctor's appointment:

- Do always ask the doctor to repeat something you don't understand.

- Do always ask for the nurse's name and the secretary's name, and write them down in your notebook.

- Do always make sure to find out the calling hours.

- Do always take notes when the doctor is talking to you.

- Do ask for literature or any information to help you understand a procedure or help you familiarize yourself with the condition.

- Do ask for future appointments if there is a day of the week or time of the day that is less crowded.

- Do request to be placed on a waiting list and notified of a cancellation. This can reduce the waiting time for a nonemergency appointment.

The Hospital Stay

Up to this point, we have dealt mostly with the doctor's appointment, but this chapter is about the special needs child in the medical world, and we feel some attention should be given to hospitalization. Much of what we have stated in this chapter dealing with doctor's appointments does carry over to the hospital stay, such as making sure the special sibling is taken care of.

One major consideration that does crop up, even for the doctor's appointment, but more so for hospitalization, is preparation. As we briefly mentioned in the "Before the Appointment" section, it is crucial to make sure that children are prepared at their level. What can be explained to a teenager about a hospitalization is clearly different than what will be explained to a five-year-old. It's important, no matter what the age, to strike that perfect chord and find that perfect balance in making sure your child is aware and prepared beforehand while not alarming them.

In the case of children who need to go, as an example, for a blood test, on the one hand you want the child to understand what is going on, why the blood test is needed, perhaps how it will help determine what is wrong or check to make sure what is right, and what will be happening to the child when arriving for the test. While this might alleviate any fears, so that the unknown is made known, it may also have the child worrying for days before the blood test, which can possibly overcome everything in the child's daily life.

On the other hand, not to tell the child can have a negative impact on the child. If the child shows up for the test and is totally traumatized by the needle and the laboratory, this can leave a lasting impression that may make future blood tests or other kinds of tests even more difficult. Perhaps if this child had been prepared, the trauma might not have occurred. We don't think there is a magic answer; the key is to know your child and talk it over with a support person such as a psychologist, who can best advise you what to do.

How much to prepare your child for hospitalization, when, and at what levels—these issues can only be resolved by knowing your own child and knowing the best route to pursue. Here, too, a professional can best guide you on how to handle the situation. Perhaps your child will benefit greatly by going to the hospital, seeing the environment, visiting other patients, etc. Or perhaps this step might be more detrimental than helpful to your particular child. Seek professional help, whether privately or asking the doctor hospitalizing the child, to give you the best advice for your child's particular needs.

Here is our list of do's for hospital stays:

- Do pack your child's special dolls, stuffed animals, etc.
- Do engage your child and the special sibling in as much of the decision making as possible.
- Do make sure the sibling's activities stay as routine as possible.
- Do make sure that if your child wants lots of visitors, you make people aware of the stay.
- Do have your child talk to other children for support.
- Do consult some professional, privately or through the hospital, as to the best preparation strategies.

Other Strategies

The special needs child in the medical world may have a lifestyle that includes regular routines, such as physical therapy every week, or occupational therapy, or the psychologist, speech therapy, etc. These become part of the lifestyle, like a dance lesson or any other routine that is built into the daily or weekly plan. Here, too, we can offer you strategies that can make this part of your life smoother.

One idea is to use this time as an opportunity to include the sibling. If you don't need to stay at the appointment, spend some time alone with the siblings(s). There are a variety of activities you can do depending on the area and the age of the sibling. Going for a walk, running errands, or even bringing a game to play in the waiting room are all possibilities. Helping the sibling with homework and reading the sibling a book are other possibilities and are obviously age-related. Here is a time to talk, to be alone and away from the special needs child, to spend some quality time so the special sibling will feel taken care of. It is a chance to discuss any thoughts or feelings that might crop up. You can develop your own special routine; for example, every time you take the special needs child to the therapist, it can also be your private time to do something with the sibling.

Ask the physical therapist or whomever the special needs child is visiting to allow the special sibling to join them. This experience can answer many questions for the special sibling, who might be wondering just what goes on behind those closed doors. This can help reduce some of the mystery and perhaps alleviate fears that the special sibling might be experiencing. For example, the words "physical therapy" might otherwise conjure up scary images, but if the special sibling can observe and/or participate in the procedure, then fears may be erased. It can also give the special sibling a better understanding of special needs. It can give the special needs child and the special sibling some quality bonding time together, and the sibling can feel like a helpful contributor to the well-being of his or her sister or brother.

Conclusion

In dealing with many appointments, there are inevitably many forms, and within these forms can be repeated questions. The information that is required sometimes needs research to find out when, where, etc. It is a good idea to keep a base sheet in your files to refer to.

Sandy: When Rayna was first diagnosed, all the doctors kept asking where she did what first, when she walked and talked, etc. If you keep all these standard answers in one area on one page, you always have it readily available to present whenever asked. To first get this all together, I had to refer back to the baby book for specifics. Some of the information was more immediate in my memory than others. Her first step is something I will always remember almost to the minute, but other information is written down and needs to be referred to. Putting it all together on one sheet makes it easier every time you are asked for this information.

Medical issues may be present from the beginning, or they may surface later in a child's life. Sometimes the medical issues may not be related at all to your child's special needs. Nevertheless, medical situations in and of themselves can cause anxiety and wreak havoc in a family. Hopefully, the information in this chapter will prepare you to handle the medical world, decreasing some of your difficulties and maximizing your focus and ability to cope.

6

The Special Needs Child in Education

Preparing yourself to access education services requires knowledge of the laws and regulations governing referral, identification, placement, services, and other areas that impact special education. In this chapter, we will try to provide you with some basic information regarding these laws and regulations, and we'll try to highlight some facts that parents need to be aware of.

In no way is this chapter to be viewed as a thorough legal interpretation of the laws and regulations. Our intent is to give parents some general idea of what they may experience if their child is referred for a special education evaluation or is found to have special needs, but in no way do we provide an exhaustive and detailed coverage of the regulations, which would be beyond the scope of this book. Furthermore, rules and regulations tend to change over time in response to political, economical, and social factors, and laws and regulations governing special education differ from state to state. Most of our experience has been with the Commonwealth of Massachusetts, which is somewhat different from other states; thus, we have tried to omit procedures that are mandated in Massachusetts but differ from those mandated by federal laws and regulations. We are parents, not legal experts, and we encourage you to consult legal experts if you have specific questions or concerns regarding your child and the applicable regulations in your community.

To serve a wider section of the population, the information we provide will largely reflect federal regulations. Parents need to be aware, though, that there will be variations among states, since states are allowed to provide services that go beyond those delineated in the federal regulations, though they are not allowed to contradict, nor offer less than what the federal regulations stipulate. If you have any specific questions regarding discrepancies between some of the general information we present and what you are experiencing within your school system, we recommend that you contact your State Department of Education to obtain information on state regulations and parents' rights. Another source of information may be a local advisory council or advocacy center.

For information and printed material regarding federal regulations, you can contact the Office of Special Education Programs, Department of Education, 400 Maryland Avenue SW, Switzer Building, Room 3615, Washington, D.C. 20202-2720. The telephone number is (202) 205-8825. Hearing impaired or deaf individuals may call (202) 205-9090 for TDD services. Federal regulations governing the provision of services to students with disabilities are at the 34 CFR of Federal Regulations Part 300. Part 301 addresses preschool.

Before Starting School (Birth to Age Three)

Early Intervention

If your child is identified as or suspected of having a special need between birth and age three, it is a good idea to have your child evaluated. This evaluation is conducted by a multidisciplinary team, referred to most often as the early intervention team. The team will talk with you about your concerns and evaluate your child's needs. If your child is found to be eligible for services, you and the team will develop an individualized family service plan (IFSP), which sets out the team's goals and the services and supports that will be provided to help reach those goals. The program is family-centered and community-based, and it seeks to assist families in providing the best possible care to support their children's growth and development.

Anyone with a concern about a child's development (for example, walking, talking, seeing, or behavior) in the first three years can make a referral to early intervention services. Most states have an 800 telephone number to locate the services near your home.

After Starting School

Before an Individualized Education Plan (IEP) Meeting

If your child is suspected of having a special need while already attending school, a referral for an evaluation is the first step to be taken. This referral can be initiated by parents, teachers, or other professionals. Parents must be notified that a referral has been made. Under federal regulations, a referral does not mean the child will automatically be evaluated. After a referral is made, the evaluation team will review the information to decide if an evaluation is required and what type of evaluation is necessary. The kind of assessments conducted will depend on the suspected area of special need. The purpose of the evaluation is to ascertain whether a child has a disability, and if so, what kind. Appropriate programs and services are then determined.

If it is decided that an evaluation is appropriate, the school must first obtain parental consent as required by federal regulations. If the parents refuse to grant consent, then, as a general rule, the state may take steps to challenge them. If the parents consent, or if consent is obtained otherwise by the school, the evaluation will begin. If it is decided by the evaluation team that an evaluation is not warranted, parents must be notified of that decision. The notification must also inform parents what procedural protections are available to them, in case the parents disagree with the team's decision and wish to contest it. (Refer to the "Procedural Safeguards" section just below).

Under federal regulations, the definition of *consent* includes some specific points, such as:

- The parents have been notified of all information that requires their consent.
- The information is given in the native language or other mode of communication of the parent.
- The parents agree in writing.

- The parents have been given a list of the child's records that can be released and a list of who will have access to those records.
- The parents have a clear understanding that consent is voluntary and can be revoked at any time.

Procedural Safeguards

Procedural safeguards are the safety nets that have been developed at every stage of the process to make sure that parents are involved in decisions being made on behalf of the child. Parents need to be aware of the following safeguards.

Written notices to parents are required for various situations. For example: before schools can propose or refuse to initiate or change the identification, evaluation, or placement of a child, they must first notify the parents in writing. Some of the requirements regarding notices are:

- They must be written in language that is easy to understand.
- They must be written in the native language of the parents or other mode of communication used by the parents (for example, sign language), unless it can be established that it is not feasible to do so.
- If the native language of the parents or other mode of communication used by the parent is not a written language, the school needs to make sure that the notices are translated and that the parents understand the information presented in the notices. Schools are required to document how they meet this requirement.
- An explanation of the procedural safeguards must be available to parents.

- The notice must describe what the school proposes or refuses to do and why. It must also describe the options considered by the school and why they were rejected and include a description of any other relevant factors that influenced the school's decision.

Parental consent is required at different times, such as for an initial preplacement evaluation, initial placement in a special education program, and before any personally identifiable information is disclosed. Though parental consent is required at these times, federal regulations state that this consent is voluntary and parents have a right to revoke their consent at any time.

Parents have a right to inspect and review the educational records of their child. Once a parent makes this request, the information should be provided promptly, and in any event, under federal regulations, no later than 45 days. It is always wise to put your request to inspect or review records in writing, so you have some documentation of your request. If parents come across information that they believe is inaccurate or misleading, the parents can request that the school remove this information. The school may disagree with the parents' opinion and refuse to remove the information, but it must give the parents information regarding their rights to a hearing on this matter. When information on a child's record is no longer needed for the child's education, the parents have a right to request that this information be destroyed.

Parents have the right to disagree and challenge the school on various matters, such as a school's proposal or refusal to initiate the identification, evaluation, or educational placement of a child.

Parents have a right to request an independent evaluation at the school's expense if they do not agree with the results of the school's evaluation team. An independent evaluation is one that is performed by a professional who is not a member of the school's evaluation team. Parents may also pay for an independent evaluation, the results of which must be considered by the child's school in the development of his IEP.

Parents may request mediation or a due process hearing if they cannot reach an agreement with the school over services or programming for their child.

Schools must send notification to parents regarding initiation or refusal of services, and those notices must provide parents with specific and detailed information. In other words, a school must keep parents informed as well as provide them the opportunity to disagree with or question the school's actions. Parental participation in the realm of special education commences the moment there is a suspicion of special needs, and it gains momentum during the IEP meeting. The momentum and intensity of involvement that needs to be sustained by parents may depend on variables, such as the severity of a child's special needs, the extent or type of required services, the availability of the services within the neighborhood school or community, and the type of communication that the school and the parents are able to establish, to name a few.

Preparing for an Evaluation

Once a referral is made and parents consent to an evaluation, the child should be told by the parent(s) about the testing and the purpose of the evaluation. In many school systems, the child might be evaluated by the school's multidisciplinary team (which might include, for example, the school psychologist, school counselor, reading specialist, social worker, speech and language therapist, etc.). These evaluations are usually administered during the child's school hours and will be scheduled by the evaluation team members. The child should be made aware that different adults will come to see him and might invite him to a quiet room in the school. In that room, the child will be asked to do different things, for example, work on certain activities, answer questions, draw pictures, work on puzzles, read some words or paragraphs, etc. The child may find some of the activities to be easy and others difficult, and he needs to know that is okay. Reassure the child that he is not expected to know everything, which is why they are testing him, to find out what is easy and is difficult for him.

A social history or home assessment is usually done. Though this is not required by federal regulations, evaluations usually include this type of assessment. Sometimes a school social worker will schedule a meeting and come to your home to do a home assessment. The social worker will ask about your child's developmental history and milestones, medical history, and for any information that may assist them to better understand your child and family.

Once an evaluation has been completed, the evaluation team determines if a child is eligible for special education; if the child is found to be eligible, a meeting to develop an IEP must be scheduled. In some states, meetings for determining eligibility and meetings for developing an IEP are held separately; in other states, these meetings are combined. If the meetings are held separately and it is determined that the child is not eligible to receive special education services, then the parents must be notified. If there are separate meetings and the child is eligible for special education, then placement decisions will be made at the IEP meeting.

Federal law requires that schools take steps to ensure parental participation in any meeting that deals with developing, reviewing, or revising a child's IEP. To assure parental participation, schools are required to pursue various steps, including the following:

- Parents must be notified of the meeting early enough to allow them an opportunity to attend.
- Meetings must be scheduled at a mutually agreed time and place.
- The notice sent to the parents must include information regarding the purpose, time, and location of the meeting, as well as information on who will be present.
- In situations where parents cannot attend the meeting, the school needs to find other ways of providing parents an opportunity to participate in the process, including individual or conference calls.
- If the school cannot convince the parents to attend a meeting, the school can then proceed with the meeting. The school is required to document its attempt to convince the parents to attend.
- Schools need to take "whatever action is necessary to ensure that parents understand the proceedings at a meeting, including arranging for an interpreter for parents who are deaf or whose native language is other than English."
- When a parent is notified of a meeting to consider transition services (see Transition Services later this chapter) the notice must indicate the purpose of the meeting, it must indicate that the school is inviting the

child to attend the meeting, and it must give the name of any other agency that has been invited to have a representative in this meeting.

- Before any IEP meetings, schools should inform parents that they can bring the child to the meeting to participate in this process.

Preparing for an IEP Meeting

To prepare yourself for an IEP meeting, you may want to speak to another parent who has gone through the experience, who may help answer any questions you might have. You are entitled to bring anyone you feel would be helpful to have there. Many parents feel more comfortable at these meetings if they can bring along a professional advocate, a friend, or another family member who may help them understand and process the information presented during the meeting. If you think you need someone to accompany you, see if the person is available for the meeting, or if not, ask if that person can share some tips with you prior to the meeting.

Bring some paper and a pencil so that you can take notes. Even though you can request copies of the evaluations, you may want to jot down information and comments as they are summarized during the meeting. These notes might be helpful after the meeting to clarify the written reports, or they may assist you in framing questions about something you are not clear on or with which you disagree. If the evaluations are ready prior to the IEP meeting, request to see them. If you have an opportunity to familiarize yourself with the findings of the assessment prior to the IEP meeting, you will be able to ask specific questions and you might feel better prepared to discuss and decide on placement decisions.

Also, take some time to write down, from your perspective, a list of the child's strengths (what he does well) and weaknesses (what he has difficulty with). Write down how you would like your child to be helped, what kind of assistance you may need as a parent or as a family, your goals for your child, and any other questions that might pop into your head. During the IEP meeting, many of your questions or concerns should be addressed, but if they are not, your notes will remind you of topics you need to raise and that you feel need to be addressed prior to the development of the child's IEP.

During the IEP Meeting

An IEP meeting can be a rather intimidating experience, but it can be somewhat ameliorated by having an idea of what will take place.

At an initial meeting to develop an IEP and determine placement, the members of the multidisciplinary evaluation team might be there to give a summary of their evaluations and findings, or perhaps one member of the team may be present to explain the test results and the procedures used during the evaluation. Federal regulations state a minimum of who must attend these meetings; your state may require the attendance of additional people. At a minimum, the participants at an IEP meeting must include the following:

- A school representative with the necessary qualifications to provide or supervise special education provisions; the child's teacher should not be assigned this role
- The child's teacher

- One or both parents
- When considered appropriate, the child
- Other individuals deemed appropriate by the parents or school
- For an initial evaluation: a member of the evaluation team and someone from the school (the child's teacher, a school representative, or other professional) who has knowledge about the evaluation procedures being presented and is familiar with the results
- When including transition services, the school is required to invite the student and a representative of any agency that is likely to be considered a responsible party in providing the services.

If the parents have requested an independent evaluation, they should arrange for a report to be sent to the school prior to the IEP meeting. The school must consider the findings of that evaluation when developing a child's IEP. An independent evaluator can attend the school IEP meeting at the parents' request and expense. In certain cases, having this person present might be helpful to summarize findings, share recommendations, and clarify any questions pertaining to the results of the evaluations and/or the recommendations.

An IEP must be developed before a child can be provided with special education or related services. After the IEP meeting, the IEP must be put into effect as soon as possible, thus it is required that the projected date for the initiation of services be included in the IEP. The IEP is a written commitment of the necessary resources that will enable a child with disabilities to receive special education and related services. Once the services are written in the

IEP, there is a legal obligation to provide those services to the child. These services cannot be dropped or altered unless procedural safeguards are followed beforehand.

An IEP meeting is an opportunity for parents and schools to communicate about the needs of a child. It is not permissible for schools to present a completed IEP to parents and just ask for their approval. Parents must be active and equal participants in discussing and developing an IEP. If parents are presented with a completed IEP, developed by the school's evaluation team prior to the IEP meeting, then that IEP has not been prepared in a manner that reflects federal regulations. The IEP must be developed by taking into account the findings of the multidisciplinary team, parental input, and discussion of other relevant information that may surface during the IEP meeting.

As the child's IEP is being developed, parents also need to be aware that in designing or selecting services and placements for a child, federal regulations state that schools should aim at providing those placements in the least restrictive environment, so that children with disabilities are educated, as much as possible, with children that do not have disabilities. Special education placements are designed to follow a continuum of services—from the most restrictive, which include residential classes, to the least restrictive, which can mean having the child go to a learning center to receive services or having the special education teacher come into the child's classroom to provide the services. The federal regulations also state that efforts must be made to identify the least restrictive environment in which the child should receive the necessary services.

Before the meeting ends, the parents and all those present at the meeting might be requested to sign a sheet that might later be attached to the IEP. This will document who attended the meeting and in what capacity. In some instances, parents will usually be requested to sign a sheet indicating whether they accept or reject the IEP (in some states where consent is required whenever an IEP is developed, parental signatures will be necessary). Parents should request a copy of the evaluations and the IEP so that they have an opportunity to read it, reflect on the information, and ask for any clarifications. Remember that parental consent is voluntary and can be revoked by the parent at any time. Direct services for the child should begin immediately after parents have accepted the IEP.

Disagreements between Parents and Schools

Sometimes the IEP meeting can be very tense, and consensus is not reached on the definition of the needs of the child and/or the services required by the child. Parental input does not mean that in each and every case the school will agree with the parent. In advocating for your child's services and focusing on his educational needs, it is important to look at and service the whole child. You need to look at how a child is doing socially and emotionally, and how this is linked to the child's academic progress. Educational needs do not refer only to academics. A child's educational needs also encompass related services for the child to make educational progress. These related services might include occupational therapy, speech therapy, counseling, etc. Children with special needs are entitled to receive related services that are necessary in order to benefit from the special education.

Make sure you understand why the school is refusing or rejecting the services that you are requesting. If it is related to providing a particular program, do they have a program in place with which you are not familiar? Are you requesting outside services without complete knowledge of the school program? Is what your school is offering inappropriate for your child, and do you have good documentation to support your case? What do you do? Where do you start?

Following are some possible steps to take.

Request an opportunity to visit and observe the programs that the school offers. Talk to the teachers in these programs and ask questions or raise concerns. This will give them an opportunity to address the issues that you raise.

Contact a professional advocate or legal counsel to discuss your issues and concerns. This person should be able to assist you in understanding if your requests are appropriate, if what the school is offering is inappropriate, or if the school is violating your child's rights. With this person, you might be able to examine strategies to effectively communicate with the school and explore possible assistance in the negotiation.

Explore every possible avenue and suggestion that will keep communication open and negotiations on an amicable level. Keep in mind that if you reach an impasse, you can then proceed to mediation or to a due process hearing. At the first sign of disagreement or tension, do not feel that you will only succeed by taking the school head on. Do not sit in frustration or anger, either. As stated earlier, take a proactive stance: gather information, access advice, and prepare yourself to engage in dialogue with the school in hopes of reaching an agreement and understanding. This is an instance when detailed documentation may be helpful. Keeping information and incidents clearly organized can assist you during contacts with the school or during a hearing if your case moves in that direction. Also, remember to consider an independent evaluation.

If, during an initial IEP meeting, the parents and the school do not reach a consensus or if there are any disputes, then as a general rule schools and parents may agree to an interim course of action that would remain in place until both parties can resolve their disagreements over the IEP. If the parents and the school cannot agree on an interim program, the child is to remain in the regular program until the issues are resolved. If the child already has an IEP, and the disagreements are over placement or services in the new IEP being developed, the child has a right to remain in the last agreed-upon placement, pending the outcome of a hearing, or until the parents and the school agree on a different arrangement. If the parents request a hearing on issues where there is disagreement, the child has a right to continue to receive the services specified in the last agreed-upon IEP.

There may be situations in which the school and the parents agree on most of the services the child needs to receive but do not agree on a specific related service. In such cases, the U.S. Department of Education's interpretation of federal regulations recommends that the IEP be implemented in all of the areas where there is agreement; that areas of disagreement be indicated on the IEP; and that steps be taken to resolve the disagreement(s).

In situations where the school and the parents are not in agreement over the placement or kind of special education to be provided, the following steps can be considered by the school:

- Tell parents that they have a right to resolve the issues by following the due process procedures.
- Try to develop an interim program that both the school and the parents can accept and that would remain in place until the disagreement is resolved.

- Recommend the use of mediation to see if the disagreement can be resolved without going to a due process hearing.

As a general rule, states offer parents and school districts the right to request mediation as a way to resolve a disagreement over services/and or placement. These meetings are encouraged by federal law but are not required by it. If the disagreement cannot be resolved during mediation, the parents can then request a due process hearing. Parents can request or go to a hearing without mediation, and they can ask for mediation after a hearing.

The law provides the parent with the right to a due process hearing when there is a dispute over any aspect of the child's placement. Due process is an independent (from the school) and formal hearing. This meeting is presided over by an appointed officer who hears evidence, information from the parents' and the school's perspectives, and then rules on the case. A hearing can be long and detailed. The parents have a right to counsel, but at their own expense. If the hearing officer rulers in favor of the parents, though, they are entitled to recover the lawyer's fees from the school.

After the IEP Meeting

As you think about the information presented and discussed during the IEP meeting and go over the notes you took and/or the copies you received on the evaluations performed, you might think of many questions you wish that you had asked. You may say to yourself, "Why didn't I ask for clarification if I was not sure I understood what they were saying?" and there may be a tendency to come down hard on yourself for not being more assertive, for not asking enough questions, for not knowing what to ask, and so forth. Be kind to yourself. These can be very intense and emotionally charged meetings, and it may take a while for you to absorb and digest the information given to you. Also remember that it is never too late to raise questions and ask for clarification. Before you leave the meeting, ask who your contact person will be at the school or in the school system who you can call with any questions or concerns that may arise.

After an IEP meeting you may experience relief if your child's issues have been clearly defined, if you agree with the findings, if the school feels that they can handle your child's special needs and provide the necessary services, and if the program that your child requires can be provided within the neighborhood school.

Anxiety, frustration, or anger, on the other hand, can occur if you disagree with the school over the diagnosis of the child's needs and the services to be provided, if you perceive the school to be unwilling to accommodate your child's needs, if you feel as if the school is unwilling to listen to your input. Remember that you do not have to accept the IEP and that you have a right to a due process procedure to resolve the disagreements that you have with the school. Knowing that you may be headed for a period of negotiation and waiting can heighten your anger and frustration. Finding the appropriate and necessary support and advice during this period is essential.

Step back and analyze the difficulty that you are having. Is it with the assessment results, the services to be provided, the location of the services, or what? Think about your options. Do you request an independent evaluation or do you need to contact an advocate or legal counsel, or is mediation or a due process hearing in order?

Independent Evaluations

If you disagree with the assessment results, remember that parents have a right to request an independent evaluation at the school's expense and that the results of that evaluation have to be considered in the development of the child's IEP. You need to find out from your state what the timelines are for requesting an independent evaluation. Before the independent evaluation takes place, check the procedures within your school system that you must follow if you want the independent evaluation to be done at public expense. You can always obtain an independent evaluation at your own expense.

Once an independent evaluation is done, the parents will usually have a meeting with the professional who evaluated the child to discuss the findings and the recommendations. Shortly after, the parents should receive a written report of the findings. Parents should make arrangements to send a copy to the school. Remember never to send your original papers—always a copy.

After the IEP meeting, you can request a copy of the IEP for your child. According to federal law (though state laws may require other information), this document, at the minimum, should include the following information:

- A statement of the child's present levels of educational performance
- A statement of annual goals, including short-term instructional objectives
- A statement of the specific special education and related services to be provided to the child and the extent

that the child will be able to participate in regular education programs

- The projected dates for initiation of services and the anticipated duration of the services
- Appropriate objective criteria and evaluation procedures and schedules for determining, on at least an annual basis, whether the short-term instructional objectives are being achieved.

Transition Services

Information regarding transition services for a child are also to be included in the IEP, no later than by the time the child is sixteen years of age. Transition services are defined by federal law to mean "a coordinated set of activities for a student, designed within an outcome-oriented process, that promotes movement from school to post-school activities, including postsecondary education, vocational training, integrated employment (including supported employment), continuing and adult education, adult services, independent living, or community participation." Transition services can be started when the child is younger if it is decided that it is appropriate. The final determination of when to initiate transition services for students under the age of sixteen is left to the IEP process. When it is decided that a child is to receive transition services, the IEP must include the following:

- "A statement of the needed transition services, including, if appropriate, a statement of each public agency's and each participating agency's responsibility or linkages, or both, before the student leaves the school setting."

- "If the IEP team determines that services are not needed in one or more areas (specified in the law), the IEP must include a statement to that effect and the basis upon which the determination was made."

Ongoing Tasks: Keeping the Child from Falling through the Cracks

As we talk about evaluating progress, parents also need to remember that the IEP is not a contract but a written commitment of the resources that are necessary if the child is to receive a free and appropriate public education. Under the law, schools and teachers are expected to make efforts to help a child meet the goals and objectives stated in that child's IEP, but they cannot be held accountable if the child fails to meet those goals and objectives. The IEP is the educational program needed by the child that the school must provide. It is not a guarantee that the child will progress at a given rate.

This does not mean that parents do not have a right to address any issues. If the parents are not satisfied with the child's progress or with the program, they have the right to contact the school and request a review of the IEP, or they can request a due process hearing. Before you meet with the school or request a due process hearing, be sure you are clearly documenting your observations and concerns so that you can effectively state your case.

Once you have received a copy of the IEP, do not forget to file it in the appropriate place in your file system. This is a very important document.

Updating the IEP

Now that your child has an IEP and is receiving the necessary services, you may wonder how schools update the information, measure progress, and make necessary adjustments to the IEP to meet the actual needs of the child. Federal law requires annual reviews of the IEP to ensure that a child's IEP reflects the present needs of a child or that the necessary changes be made if the child's needs are not being met with the present plan. Schools are required to reevaluate the child every three years, or sooner if requested to do so by the parents.

Ongoing Communication and Coordination: The Teacher, Support Services, and the Home

An important process that needs to be cultivated is the ongoing communication between the school and the parents. It is important to share with the school any changes that occur in the family, since those changes may impact a child's behavior or academic performance. Some changes you can immediately recognize as being significant, for example, a change in medication, an illness or a death in the family, or anything else that may have an impact on the child. Other changes you might see as issues that you handle on your own and do not need to share with the school, for example, going away for the weekend, an extended visit by a grandparent, a new baby-sitter, changes in your work schedule, etc. You might actually need to share this information as well, because it might affect a child's performance and/or behavior. The teachers will be in a better position to understand your child and to assist him if they have an idea of how to interpret the child's behavior.

If a child has homework, it is a good idea to meet the teachers and clarify expectations: how much supervision the parent should provide, and how much time the child should devote to completing the assigned tasks. Here are some questions to raise with teachers if your child is having difficulty with an assignment:

- Should you try to help the child, or should you write a note to the teacher indicating the child's difficulty with the work?
- Should you let the child do the advocating for himself?
- If the child is supposed to be working for one hour on homework and he is not done during that time period, should you stop the child and write a note to the teacher, so that the teacher has a realistic indication of what the child is capable of doing on his own, including his fatigue level?

Sharing your observations about how a child does homework, organizes himself, handles frustration, problem-solving strategies, etc. can assist a teacher in pacing the work and modifying the tasks so that your child can more successfully and independently complete homework. The teacher might also be able to provide you with some suggestions to help you organize or assist your child in a manner that is conducive to his becoming as self-sufficient and independent as he is capable of being for his age and abilities.

Through dialogue with your child's teacher and counselor, you might also start to plan how to help your child to negotiate the school environment and academic demands; in other words, to teach your child how to start advocating more for himself.

If your child is having difficulties in a class or classes, share your concerns with the teachers and ask for their support and suggestions. Ask how you can help your child with the expectations from the teacher or to clarify what the expectations are. Knowing what to expect ahead of time helps parents focus on their child's performance. Your ability to pick up difficulties is thus sharpened and heightened.

By sharing your concerns ahead of time, you have alerted the teacher to keep an eye out for possible difficulties. If the child is not performing to satisfaction, the teacher is aware that it might be due to a need for intervention, support, or modification of tasks or workload, rather than making erroneous assumptions about the child's motivation or efforts.

One good rule to follow in communicating with teachers and other professionals is to apply the same principles of communication that are effective in business and personal relations. Asking rather than demanding, questioning rather than attacking, sharing rather than accusing, being assertive rather than aggressive—these qualities will make your relationship with the the educator much more harmonious.

When parents and teachers communicate on an ongoing basis, they provide the child with a consistent message of expectations, which is a steady and strong base. In addition, the child is also provided with ongoing support and encouragement that carries over from one environment to another in a consistent way. This can be very reassuring to the child. For example, you may communicate to the school that you are encouraging your child to speak up for himself and to be assertive. Having the teachers be aware of how important and/or difficult this step might be for your child might make them more able to assist and encourage him in these first attempts at asserting himself. They might also assist you by searching for, or identifying within the school, opportunities to encourage your child to put this goal into practice and provide the child with the necessary feedback for evaluation and validation.

Some teachers might find it helpful if you develop a short overview of your child's strengths and weaknesses, something that they can quickly look at that will assist them in understanding the child better. You might also want to consider developing a small information package that provides the teacher with information on your child's disability. Be selective in what you choose for the package; look for information that is easy to read and provides good information or suggestions for helping the child.

If your child is in elementary school, it might be a good idea to meet informally with your child's teacher on a regular basis. Let your child's teacher know ahead of time that you will stop by the class, just to touch base and make sure that everything is running smoothly. At that time, if the teacher feels that there is some concern or issue you need to talk about, then you will be able to schedule a meeting to discuss the matter at a mutually convenient time. This might allow you to catch a problem before it becomes a crisis. It is usually easier and faster to resolve an issue before it escalates or a pattern is established, so you want to stay on top of the situation. But you also need to be careful that you do not do it in a way that is counterproductive or offensive.

At the middle school or the high school level, it might be more difficult to keep tabs on how your child is doing because your child is taught by more than one teacher. One good contact person might be the guidance counselor. Besides providing you and your child support, the guidance counselor can indicate to you when it might be beneficial or necessary to also contact a specific teacher or the principal.

If you cannot reach a teacher by phone, put a note in the school mailbox and indicate that it is important that you meet. Include in the note at what times you are available to receive calls, and on what days and at what time you are available to meet. In other words, indicate how soon you need to meet and provide some information on your availability or flexibility.

You can also request teachers to indicate to you good days and times for you to try to contact them.

Maria: After receiving a note from me, some of my daughter's teachers will leave a message on the answering machine, telling me when they are free. When I call the school, I am usually successful in contacting the teacher because we have made this arrangement. I find that when I provide the teachers with information regarding my availability and they do the same with me, we can reduce phone tag and frustration on both sides.

In communicating with your child's teachers and school, make sure that you also provide positive feedback. If you are satisfied with the program, tell them. If you find that the school and teachers are doing a good job, thank them for their assistance and for their interest and involvement in your child's program and progress. If you feel that someone has been very helpful to you or your child, consider writing a note to the principal and/or the director of a department to acknowledge the efforts of a teacher and/or support staff. Many of these people work very hard on behalf of the children and often receive little acknowledgment for going the extra mile, for being thorough and caring, for making each child feel special even though they are responsible for many other students.

At this point, you may be asking why we are talking about setting goals and communicating with teachers if your child has an IEP with its goals and objectives documented. Remember that your child is a dynamic entity, growing and changing rapidly on an ongoing basis. You can't expect to determine and predict all of his needs at one IEP meeting and have those remain constant until the annual review. Our children sometimes surprise us by doing better than expected, or, during the course of the year, they may encounter a challenge we did not foresee. If a major need is identified that needs to be included in the IEP, you can request the IEP team to reconvene so that the IEP can be reviewed.

In certain instances, the new difficulties the child encounters during the school year can be addressed by communicating with the child's teacher and devising strategies or modifications that can easily take care of the situation. All that is really required is an understanding of the objective and an agreement to support each other. Some of these goals can be accomplished within a short period of time or within a given school year, because they are situation-specific. At the end of the school year, you and the child's teacher may decide that a goal you have been working on has not been met and should be incorporated in the IEP so that your child will continue to receive ongoing support.

Before the year-end review of the IEP, take some time to think about what your child has achieved during the school year, what are some of the areas he needs help with, and what are your goals for the next year. This is a time to listen to the school's appraisal of your child's efforts, gains, and difficulties. By sharing the home and school perspective, you are both presenting a more integrated description of the child. Remember that your child has to function in two different worlds that may at times vary in their expectations, requirements, and support. The more the teachers and parents can understand and support one another, the more the child will benefit from such collaboration. There might be times when parents need to listen to the school's goals and request for support if gains are to be made. There are also times when schools need to listen to parents and give these goals as much validity and support as those stemming from the school's perspective.

Records and Confidentiality

Somewhere along the way, there will come a time when you may wonder about your child's record and worry about what information is kept there and how your child's confidentiality is being protected. This concern is not an overreaction or an indicator of an overprotective parent. Parents do have some specific rights in this arena. To start with, parents can ask to examine and review any records kept by the school that relate to their child's identification, evaluation, and educational placement. Schools are required to make them accessible as promptly as possible. These records are also to be made available, upon the parents' request, prior to an IEP meeting or to a due process hearing.

If parents request a copy of the records, schools are permitted to charge a fee to cover the costs of copying the records, but federal regulations stipulate that this can be done as long as the fee does not prevent parents from inspecting and reviewing the given records.

If, while examining your child's records, you discover some information that seems inaccurate or misleading, you can bring it to the school's attention and request that they amend the information. If the school does not agree with the parent and refuses to amend the records, the school must inform parents promptly and advise parents that they have a right to a hearing on this matter. If at a hearing the information in question on the child's records is found to be inaccurate or misleading, the school will be required to make the necessary changes and to inform the parents in writing. If the information is not found to be inaccurate or misleading, the school then must inform the parents that they have a right to prepare a written statement, to be included in their child's record, commenting on the information that they question and explaining why they disagree with the decision to not have the information changed.

Regarding confidentiality: parents need to be aware that there are strict regulations regarding who can have access to the records or to whom those records can be released. Parental consent is required before any personally identifiable information is given to anyone outside of the school. Schools are required to protect the confidentiality of a child's records and are required by federal regulation to maintain a current listing of the names and positions of the people who may have access to a child's records. This list is to be available for public inspection.

Another question you may eventually raise regarding your child's special education records is the life span of the information. How long should these records be kept? Should they eventually be destroyed?

This information can be kept on file unless the parents communicate to the schools that they want it destroyed. Though it might be tempting to destroy such records, seek legal advice from someone with experience in protecting the rights of or in accessing services or benefits for people with disabilities. Later in a child's life, this information may be necessary in order for the child to qualify for some needed benefits or services. So do not be in a rush to destroy records without first accessing appropriate counsel on the pros and cons of this decision.

If the parents request to have the special education records destroyed, schools are permitted to keep, on a permanent basis, the following information on a student:

- Name
- Address
- Telephone number
- Grades
- Attendance records
- Classes attended
- Grade level completed
- Year completed

Conclusion

Throughout this chapter, we have tried to give you a basic understanding of the procedural rights of parents and special needs children. It is advisable that you familiarize yourself with the federal regulations if you want a thorough understanding of the law and if you want to grasp the language of the regulations. To receive a copy of the federal regulations governing special education, you may contact your state Department of Education or the Office of Special Education Programs (the address and phone numbers are provided at the beginning of this chapter).

For those of you interested in a concise version of parents' rights in the special education process, contact the state Department of Education, Division of Special Education or the office of special education of your local school district and request a brochure on parents' rights. These brochures are easy to read and understand. Every parent with a special needs child should have one.

For all children, the years in school are a significant period in their lives. This is not only a time to develop academic skills but a time to grow socially as well as emotionally. Education is the road that leads to independence, and it equips an individual to eventually contribute to the community. Children with special needs will vary in the degree of independence that they achieve and in their capacity to become active contributors in the community, nevertheless their right to an education and the opportunity to develop their maximum potential should never be curtailed.

The years that your child is in school can be fairly easygoing or intense, depending on your child's special needs and the services available within your school system. These will be years when the skills and information we present throughout the book will be most needed by parents. Because of the child's changing needs and the inevitable and ongoing transitions, parents are required to be organized and to know how to access resources and how to advocate on their child's behalf.

During these years, we are the guardians and mediators of our children. Our responsibility as parents is to make sure that our children receive the best education that they can possibly get, to supervise the process to ensure that our rights and our children's rights are being upheld, and to take action when something goes astray. It is a complex process that requires parental participation. Though procedural safeguards have been built into the process and schools have a responsibility to deliver programs and services included in the child's IEP, parents must always remain watchful and informed.

Over time, many parents find that they have become a resource for other parents. Some parents may be surprised to find themselves volunteering in various organizations or training to become certified advocates in order to further assist other parents through a course that they have traveled, to share their knowledge and understanding of the process.

Becoming familiarized with federal and state laws and regulations might seem an added burden to an already difficult situation. How thorough one becomes in this area will vary greatly among parents. We believe that parents should have some basic familiarity and understanding of their rights and where to access legal advice or professional advocacy in their community.

Remember that there are usually legal and advocacy services available to parents, and sometimes these services can be accessed for free or for a nominal fee. Research your community and state thoroughly so that you can access as much support or advice as necessary. Every state should have an office that is charged with protecting and advocating the rights of individuals with disabilities. They may provide free legal assistance regarding special education issues. Your state Department of Education should be familiar with these services and be able to provide you with information regarding their location.

Transitions

Transitioning—a word that encompasses so many arenas in life. Often we think of transitions as major events that require our attention at given times in our lives, but we fail to notice that in our daily living we are constantly facing and negotiating transitions.

Our original intent in this chapter was to address transition in the broader sense, thus organizing the topic according to major areas in the education world: transition from early intervention to preschool, elementary school, middle school, high school, and to college or vocation. We wanted to address each passage as a unique event in the child's life, looking at each aspect of the ramifications of transitioning. In doing extensive interviews, though, it became apparent that the daily, smaller, ongoing transitions that our children face could be as demanding and disruptive as the major ones; these transitions also require that we provide our child with ongoing understanding and support. Thus, before looking at major transitions that our children will encounter, we would first like to acknowledge and address some of those ongoing transitions required by daily living.

Daily Transitions

If we start thinking about all the areas in life that involve transitions, we can identify some difficulties. We may notice that when we travel or spend the day away from home, away from our normal routines, we sometimes find it difficult to jump back into the main picture, to reengage with the activities and demands we left behind. We may need time and space to reacquaint ourselves, to prepare ourselves for the shifting demands and requirements from one environment to the other.

Ongoing transitions in a child's life refer to events such as going from playing or watching TV to getting ready to go out on an errand or to school; moving from one activity in the classroom to another; moving from one classroom to another; going from a passive activity (reading a book) to an active task (going for a bike ride). For some children, these smaller, daily transitions can be difficult to negotiate. For some, even moving from room to room within the house or subject to subject while doing homework can be difficult transitions.

Being aware of transitioning issues is imperative. What could be misinterpreted as laziness or excuses for not doing homework might actually be the more serious issue of not knowing how to get started on a task or having difficulty shifting from math homework to language homework. A child might have difficulty transitioning from the dinner hour to homework time or to bedtime. The most important thing to remember is that the difficulties experienced by the child or the chaos taking place at a given time, whether from school to school, weekend to weekday, or supper to homework, might be due to transitioning issues.

Often the child cannot recognize this difficulty and cannot express it in words. This can make it harder for you to understand what is going on. "I can never seem to get Billy to settle down after dinner to do his homework." You might think a punishment is in order. "Billy, if you don't do your homework right now, you won't get to watch that show." Perhaps this can make it even more difficult for Billy to handle transition. But, if you are aware of his problems, then you as the special needs parent can help implement some strategies to help him with transition.

The strategies won't necessarily be the same for every child, and the best advice we can give you is to talk to the child's teachers or a professional and work out what will best suit your child. For some, it might be as simple as having you open the history book, look at the assignment, understand what has to be done, and get everything ready before the dinner hour, so that after dinner Billy can go do his homework with everything already in place. It might mean that you have to sit down with Billy for a minute to get him started or perhaps use a bridging activity, such as a brief walk, a game of cards, or even a television show. A kitchen timer can be helpful, as well.

Maria: After finishing one task and before starting another one, Maria Cristina often needs some quiet time. Depending on the task that she is working on, she may need five minutes or fifteen minutes. When she finishes the task at hand, she has learned to set the timer, and she uses that time to disengage from what she has just finished. When the timer rings, she goes back to her desk and is ready to start on a new assignment. The timer allows her to take some time off without losing track of time, and it also allows me to remove myself from the role of having to remind her to go back to her work and take ownership for keeping her on track. When we initially started, Maria Cristina had a difficult time knowing how much time she should allocate for transitioning, so I helped her by giving her a choice. I would say something like, "Do you need a ten or a fifteen minute break before you start your next assignment?" Now she has a good sense of the time she needs and often negotiates with herself. By that I mean that she may set the timer for twenty minutes, and after ten minutes, she feels ready and announces that she has decided to go back to finish her work. Throughout this process, Maria Cristina has been learning how to manage her time and also to feel in control of a situation.

The child's difficulty is expressed most often through frustration, anxiety, refusal, or outbursts. As parents, we need to recognize and acknowledge these ongoing transitions and how the child deals with them, if we are to successfully assist them in coping with these daily demands. We also need to help our children understand when their behavior is a manifestation of their difficulty with a transition, so they can better comprehend what is happening to them and why.

Being prepared and familiarized with the tasks that lay ahead helps us prepare ourselves for the transition. Reflect on what helps you cope with transitions, and see if these techniques can be of help to your child on different occasions. You may need an array of techniques, for some techniques will be more applicable than others depending on the situation, age of the child, the degree to which a child can tolerate transitions, and the type of transition.

In some situations, it might be appropriate and helpful to give the child a verbal indication that a change is about to take place. For example, the parent or teacher can state: "In ten minutes, we are going to start picking up our things because we are going to go to the supermarket/to the cafeteria." This allows children to slowly disengage from what they are presently doing and prepare themselves for what they need to do next. In other situations, it might be more appropriate to provide some down time. For example, when returning from a vacation, it might be helpful to return early in the day on the last day of the vacation or a day before the child is to return to school or you are to go back to work. This can provide the child some time with things that are familiar and comforting that they have missed or an opportunity to call a friend and reestablish connections—a chance to slowly ease into the routines and structures of the home before facing those of the school.

Major Transitions

With the interviews that follow, we proceed with the original intent of this chapter by focusing on some of the major transitions the child may experience during his or her lifetime. Through the following interviews with professionals and parents, we hope to provide you with information and facts that will familiarize and prepare you for these important and necessary shifts.

We asked many of the interviewees similar questions, to reveal the varying aspects and common bonds of the transition stages. For example, we asked about the questions generally asked by parents. Some of these answers were quite universal: at each stage, the parent would be concerned about the child fitting in or getting ready for the next step. Obviously, some of the concerns of a parent of a two-year-old didn't match the ones about a special needs child going off to college. The general theme that did remain constant was the importance of parents anticipating events and issues long before the necessity of dealing with them, asking questions and seeking advice prior to facing the task. This by itself says something about special needs parents: we are concerned, we think ahead, we attempt to anticipate the obstacles (in fact, we seem to desperately need to know what the obstacles will be and are frustrated when we can't).

Our purpose in doing these interviews was twofold:

- To help you once again eliminate or decrease those feelings of isolation. Reading professional answers to some of the questions that you might have gives you that identifying support, so you know that you are not the only parent feeling this way.
- To give you a better understanding of what does happen each step along the way in preparing your child for the next school.

We present these interviews in the chronological order of the transition, up to the child graduating high school. You can read them from beginning to end, or you can read about the stage that your child is at—whatever you feel will be the most useful. If you do choose to jump ahead to your child's level, we recommend that you go back and read the other interviews as well, to give you a general sense of the different stages and to give you a better understanding of what your child faced in the past.

Certain terms used in these interviews are not necessarily terms encountered in the federal regulations but are specific to the particular state in which the interviewed person resides. These include the following:

- Chapter 766 refers to the Special Education Law in Massachusetts.
- Team meetings refer to evaluation and IEP meetings that are conducted as one meeting.
- Core is the term used interchangeably with team or IEP meetings.

About Transitions

First, we interviewed a social worker who specializes in support groups for children with special needs. This will give you an overview of transitioning, then we'll move on to the various levels.

What do you think are some of the best ways to assist the special needs child facing transitions?

In general, I find there are two key tools in assisting the special needs child with transitions: risk taking and opportunities for decision making. In early childhood, games and fun activities prepare the child to take risks. I encourage children to be open to trying new experiences and new opportunities, whether it's a new game, a new way to play the game, or even trying a new unfamiliar food. For some children, too much stimuli and noise can be a paralyzing experience, such as the open, noisy cafeteria or the changing of classes in the hallway.

One way to build up confidence in risk taking is to do things differently in a variety of experiences. For example, having a job at home that can be accomplished gives children a chance to feel capable of completing tasks. Another way to teach a child to take risks is to allow a child to begin to select his own clothes. This actually spills over into the other area, decision making. Taking risks and decision making are not mutually exclusive concepts. Deciding which clothes to wear and taking the risk of doing it as an independent activity complement one another in the enhancement of the child's confidence-building skills. I truly believe these are strong foundations that can help later in the transitioning processes. Remember that transitioning is not necessarily confined to schools but from one year to the next, from Friday to Monday, and from one stage of life to the next. Life in itself is a series of transitions.

What are common needs of the students?

When looking at transitions, we need to focus on the personality structure of the child involved. This information must be integrated into the process of transition. Conflicts can arise when you have very flexible parents and a very rigid child, and vice versa. If these factors are not addressed and considered in the preparation, you may not be giving the child the necessary support. Another example of taking the personality of the child into consideration is dealing with the child who has dealt with any trauma, especially medical. In many cases, this plays a major role in how a child handles transitions, for the question of trust plays a prominent role. For some children it might mean having trouble establishing trust with authority figures, while for other children relating to adults may be very comfortable and reassuring. We need to understand each child's history and what is comfortable for each child in dealing with transitions. Parents sometimes don't take time to think about that.

There are different tasks and activities to assist with separation. For example, with a very young child, drawing a picture of a family member on each fingertip can make a child feel connected while venturing out into a new world. These pictures can serve as transition objects and reassure children that their family is still with them, diminishing the isolation factor. For older children who make lots of transitions during the week from day care to baby-sitters or after-school programs, rigidity can occur, and these children can get very confused as to where they are supposed to go, who will be driving them, etc. One method to help the child in this scenario is to use an index card with schedules spelled out and emergency numbers available, so that a child can feel more connected. Tucked inside a lunch box, the card can clarify, reassure, and comfort.

What roles do parents and educators play in transitioning?

Parents and educators have to work as a team. This works better in some environments than in others. Some environments are set up more rigidly than others, and this can be challenging. While some caretakers are very adaptable and warm and can be interested in the various learning styles of the kids, others are not. Their attitude is "This is how we do it," or "This is how it is done here." As children get older and the settings change, more emphasis needs to be placed on preparation. "What does my child need?" "What is the school capable of doing?" "What do I need to know?" These are questions parents constantly ask. For many kids, not knowing can be terrifying.

At what period of their lives do children tend to have more problems with transitions?

I don't find problems to be prevalent in one particular age more than another. It hooks into the self-confidence of the child. Some children acquire this at a very early age, and others don't feel self-confident until high school or beyond. Not knowing is very difficult for children as well as disruptions of their routines. For example, a younger child may have difficulty riding on a bus and not being sure whether to get off or dealing with the pecking order of older students on the bus.

Children may have perceptions and fears of a situation and not know how to express them. It is crucial as a parent to be aware of this need and to ask a child, "What can I do to help?" "What is on your mind?" Children also have issues of independence, especially from middle school on, and this is particularly true with special needs children who have always needed extra support along the way. At this stage, many try to fight the label of special education, not wanting to be identified as different.

What are some suggestions for parents?

Kids need to come to terms with who they are, including their strengths and their weaknesses. Let them know that everybody has weaknesses. Another suggestion is to teach the child how to access the system. Though schools may have difficulty getting involved with children before the actual start of the school year, it may be important for a special needs child to find or meet significant adults they will be working with in the year to come. Children in fifth and sixth grade should be involved in the evaluation process. This teaches them how to negotiate and minimizes dependency on the parent, which is the breaking-away process that will be so crucial as they enter the world on their own, reaching adulthood.

If a child is prepared and has made a smooth transition from one school to the next, does this ensure that the next transition will be easier?

In a word, no. Children are influenced by the educational process. For example, in elementary school, a child may have had a good support system, and this may not carry through to the next level. Also, developmentally, one must ask what demands and attitudes are expected of the child. In high school, maturation and tools that have been gained along the way may be appropriate and the child, in fact, may be ready to do a fine job, yet when he looks around at the new environment and compares himself to peers, his confidence may be shaken. This can impact negatively on feelings of succeeding in the transition. It takes a lot of advocacy on the parent's part to assist a teacher in understanding the specific needs of some of the new students. Suggestions on how to handle a child can help smooth the way for both teacher and student.

What are some of the more common concerns of the children that you get in the support group?

Children tend to be concerned with "Will I be okay?" They don't want to be different, and they are tired of having to work harder at things and that things don't come easily. They also want to have a sense of managing their own lives. The biggest problem in early adolescence is not just the learning disabilities, but the lack of organizational skills as well. In middle school, they are negotiating with many people, usually in bigger settings, and the system can be less sympathetic. There are more restrictions in the middle school settings. People are more concerned with problems in adolescence, so there is less time to move around. For example, kids who can't hold onto information need to decide whether they stop to ask the teacher for clarification and risk being late for the next class or just rush to make their next class.

Do you have any suggestions for the child who is having a difficult time adjusting?

It will depend on each individual child. Some kids may waste time for a while. We must look back to see if there is a pattern that has emerged through the years. For example, some children may be slow in adjusting, but that is the norm for them; they need time. As parents, we must be aware of whether the child is developmentally ready for the new setting. Some kids need to have routines maintained during the summer. Consistency in their lives can help, so as not to lose ground. For example, you can have them do a supermarket list, so they can practice their writing skills. The older student could keep a journal during the summer. Parents should also encourage reading. People need to respect kids and what they need to feel comfortable. It's important to listen to the child. Remember that parents give off cues and children will pick up on these cues. For example, if a parent had a difficult time in transitioning to high school and shares those feelings, the child may pick up on them and have negative preconceived notions in his expectations.

Don't negate a child's right to feel anxiety. Don't say "Oh, you will be all right." Do reflective listening, i.e., give back or repeat to the child what he is saying and don't say that you will make it better.

Is there a difference in transitioning from public to private school?

It depends on the reason for changing. If the child feels that he hasn't measured up, that he has failed, this may have a negative impact on transition.

Early Intervention

Interviews with a Program Director and Program Coordinator.

Could you clarify what early intervention means?

Early intervention provides educational, therapeutic, and support services for children from birth to age three, who are either at risk for delay in development or who are currently displaying delays, as well as their families.

What makes a child eligible for early intervention?

There are three categories for eligibility: established risk, biological risk, or environmental risk. Established risk means that the child is showing developmental delay in one or more areas. Biological risk means that the child has a health or medical condition that may lead to delay, and environmental risk is the delay in development because of factors in the environment, such as substance abuse, mental health, homelessness, socioeconomic problems, or lack of appropriate shelter for the child.

How do you get the referrals?

Mostly from the families, hospitals, and doctors.

Let's move on to transitioning. When do you begin to start transitioning the child for the next school?

At age two and a half, we begin to talk with the parents and give the appropriate places to start looking at providing. We give them the name of the preschool special needs coordinator for the particular town they are going to. We share our recommendations.

Do you find the parents receptive to this or anxious?

What happens more often than not is that the parents approach us to start talking about transition long before the age of two and a half. They are worried about not getting into a private nursery school if that is the route they have decided to take, so they want to know if they should be putting deposits down a year earlier. It is very hard to know what to do—so much can change developmentally in one year, and it's hard to say whether the child will be able to go on to a private nursery school or really belongs in a public one.

Different parents react to the situations in different ways. Some parents have a hard time dealing with the fact that their child may not be going off to the same school as another sibling or siblings, or some would like their child to go to a nursery school affiliated with a religion. Part of this reaction is related to the acceptance process of accepting that your child does have a special need and it may be more long-term than just three years. These parents are just at the beginning of the education process for their child as well as the life span. We are dealing with the first three years of life, and the diagnosis can still be very new and fresh and difficult to process. So, we are dealing with more than just the child, but the parents as well.

Is it just because they want their child at a particular school?

No, there is also the stigma that some parents believe is attached to the label of special needs. Being part of the special education system can put parents on the edge, and they would prefer to keep it as quiet as possible. This is one of the reasons some parents prefer to do private testing even though they are eligible for it from the system.

Let's get back to transitioning issues and the time factor involved. What are some other considerations?

Time is a big factor. Sometimes we don't even get a child in here until the age of two or two and a half, just about the time we are endeavoring to transition them out of here, since three is the cutoff. We are simultaneously trying to settle the child in while at the same time trying to transition him out. It is a precarious balance.

What are some of the steps you take?

Well, the first is the obvious: identifying the child's special needs. Chapter 766 (the name of a special education law in Massachusetts) preschools develop an IEP by working with the parents and doing assessments or a combination of both early intervention and the school system working side by side and both doing the evaluation. Then they call a team meeting. We discuss the child's needs. A public school coordinator from preschool will make a recommendation for the child.

What are some other transitioning issues?

Another major issue is the transition from the home to the outside environment. A lot of early intervention takes place in the home, so not only are we transitioning from one type of "school" to another such as in middle to high school, we are actually transitioning to completely different types of environments. Early intervention is very family-oriented, which is different than the schools, which are education-oriented. The families have been accustomed to a lot of one-on-one situations, assistance, support, and information from early intervention. They rely heavily on us through these first few years. The transition to preschool is especially hard because it is such a different orientation, especially for the parents. It is a real letting-go process. We are transitioning the parents as well as the child. The transitioning adjustment is definitely exacerbated by concerns of separation.

Each family has a service coordinator who will go with the family to observe different programs. They will also attend the team meetings.

Transitioning is such an ongoing process, it doesn't stop the day you put the child in the program. In short, early intervention is the genesis, and it is intensified by the bonds with the family. Some of the facilitators have actually "grown up" with the child's problems, perhaps even been in on the initial diagnosis.

That sounds pretty intense, like they could be considered the savior or the enemy.

Exactly. We take the families by the hand and walk them through the whole process of transitioning to the public school. We are actually natural advocates for the parents.

What happens after they leave you? Do you keep in touch?

Many people still keep in touch. We get some visits, but more phone calls. Although there is no formal relationship after the age of three, many keep in touch and don't sever the ties altogether. I think some of the visits aren't just for information, but for security as well.

Preschool

*Interview with a Director of a Preschool Program
Funded by the State for Special Education*

Could we start with some general thoughts about transitioning to a preschool?

The most prevalent concept I can think of is the transition from a home environment to a public environment. What I mean by that is that most children in early intervention have been having lots of services at home, and it is quite a shock to go from this one-on-one environment to a school environment. The family is still dealing with the grief that the child has a problem. In many cases, the parents are still in denial. Some are still very angry. The early intervention experience is more like an extended family, and it is very difficult for the parent to go from this individualized nurturing environment to the "formal" school environment. School is a new world to any child, but it's a very new world to the special needs child because of what the child has encountered. The parents are afraid that the goals set up for the child that have been met with a one-to-one environment will not be fulfilled in the school environment. We know that the goals will be met, but it is difficult for the parents to believe this. The parents are afraid that the school will not know the child and not be able to incorporate the child into the school. Basically, the child is stepping into a big, frightening new world.

How does the transitioning process begin?

Well, let me start with how the children come here.

You mean from early intervention?

Right. The first thing we do, which is what I am sure every school does for transitioning, is sit down to get the individualized education plan, the IEP. The early intervention team recommends the times needed for support services, and they look at what the needs are of the child to accomplish their goals. What we usually run up against, as I stated before, is that the parents have this feeling that when professionals work in a one-on-one situation with the child, they will be able to "fix" what's wrong. The parents have a difficult time seeing ahead to the child being in a group.

How do you help these parents?

I tell them to go observe the different nursery schools, which include public ones such as mine and the private ones. I tell them to look at the goals and objectives. Remember, we might still be working with a parent in the grieving stage. This is a very tender stage we are talking about. The parents are going through a letting-go process. There are natural parent issues as it is; couple this with special needs, and it can be difficult. In a sense, they are mixing developmental issues with special needs issues, and while no one can predict the future, it is hard to project the child's long-term needs.

Do all parents experience this?

No. There is the other extreme of the parent that drops the kid off and says, "You fix it, you take care of it."

Do you recommend schools to the parents when they are considering a public nursery?

I talk with the parents and the early intervention people and get some sense of the level of the special needs child, which helps me decide where to place them. Sometimes the parent places the child in a regular preschool and then uses our services for physical therapy and/or occupational therapy, speech, etc.

Okay, let's talk about going from a public, core preschool such as yours to kindergarten.

The spring before the child is to enter kindergarten, the team meeting takes place. It's like a hand-over-hand transfer. We call in the specialist from the entering school to help as a liaison for the transition. This is for the more mild special needs. For the moderate-to-severe kids, we give a list to the elementary schools and discuss whether a home school or another one out of district is appropriate to meet the needs. We try to give a clear picture and once again encourage lots of observation. We need to start early so the parent can start preparing, because there are so many options. The preschool teachers meet with the parents before the kindergarten meeting to go over what will happen at the core. It's like a pre-core, giving parents and teachers an opportunity to get ready.

What next?

Well, then we have a follow-up after the team meeting. The home school attends the team meeting to help with the decision. The child needs to feel that he is welcome at the home school if that is what is selected. It's not like a test—every home school accepts the child—it's more a question of what is best for the child. The city, state, and federal government have the expectation that there is a place for any child in the public school.

Any closing thoughts?

In my opinion, this is the biggest transition: leaving the nest, the first big time, off to kindergarten. While each transition has its challenges and adjustments, I truly believe this is the number one biggest.

Interview with a Private Preschool Teacher and Director

Can you give me a general overview of transitioning? Then we'll get into some more specifics.

The most important aspect of transitioning a child from preschool to kindergarten is open lines of communication, especially before the school year begins. It might be in a written or verbal form, but the bottom line is some connection bridging the two settings. Oftentimes, we are able to contact someone from the kindergarten to come to the nursery school to observe the child. This is usually done if the child is already on an IEP, but it is also done if the child hasn't been evaluated yet. What I find really helpful for the parents is to be the child's advocate in every way possible. For instance, the parents should go to the new setting and suggest to the teacher what the child's needs are. Say something such as, "This worked in this setting, maybe you'd like to give it a try in this setting . . ."

When you start with the child at this young level being diagnosed as special needs, you are also starting with parents who are usually not familiar with the whole system, so you have to educate the parents and train them to advocate, as I suggested with that example before. You have to educate the parents on new vocabulary words, that's why it's good you've included a glossary in this book. I find also that parents don't even know how to read an IEP. We end up reading them together, and I teach them how to read one.

We seem to be getting off the track of transitioning to schools, rather talking about transitioning from home to school.

You're right, this is a different kind of transitioning. These children have never been in a setting with other children their age. We are often in the discovery part of the process.

How?

What happens is that a child comes to our program. We spend the first month observing everyone. At the end of the month, we sit down—by we, I mean all the teachers that I have had observing the class, myself as the head teacher and administrator and my assistant teachers. It's very important to have many pairs of eyes on these children, because what might not jump out for me will jump out at another teacher or observer in a different way. So, at the end of the month, we sit down as a team and share our observations and sift out the different aspects of the children. We have to decide if the behaviors we have observed are because the child is in a new environment or a new classroom, or something isn't quite in synch. They need this month for settling down, so that's why we wait. By then, children get their patterns and rituals, and we can isolate the ones that don't quite adjust like the others, something doesn't quite feel right. This is sometimes the first opportunity to have the child with other children, so we have to make sure what is wrong and what is adjustment to a new environment. So, we give it a month. Children are feeling out their new world and making new choices, and sometimes a problem can be very camouflaged. They are transitioning and we are observing this. We have to know what we are observing.

How do you sense if there is a problem or if it's just transitioning?

The emotional and social issues will usually surface first. The physical will be harder to spot, as well as the language problems. The fine motor skills are also harder to identify. What's interesting about a preschool is that the child doesn't see himself as doing something different from the others, because there are enough opportunities to do different things in the school. What's nice about this process is that there is a lot of integration and work with the child who doesn't have to be singled out. The negative is that we might not see the problem right away.

What's the hardest for the parents?

It's a new environment. Just adjusting to that transition can be a lot for all parents, then to be informed that we think the child has some special needs makes it even more monumental. Preschool is a new experience. The parents have to be trained at the outset, not just the child.

What kinds of help do the parents ask for?

A lot of the time, if they are seeking help, it's in support services. "Who can I turn to?" is often asked. The therapist helps them paint a broader picture. I help transfer them to the support system. Lots of times, parents will get advice, then call us.

What about when the child leaves here?

The parents start asking us, "What is going to happen to my child the first day of school?" The parents are usually worried about their child being isolated or singled out. Some parents have a tendency to leave all the problem solving up to the school, but these parents must be aware that they have to stay in touch and have to stay on top of it.

As a teacher, we must keep constant documentation, so that a parent can never accuse us that we never told the parent any of our observations. We are, in a sense, mandated reporters.

Some parents go to the city school and ask for a core. They are anxious and don't want their kids labeled. Some go for evaluations privately. The educational community has to be sensitive to this. The city is going to retest anyhow. They won't accept any outside testing.

We go to the core evaluation in the public school so that we can help.

Ninety-five percent of the parents don't believe what the teacher is telling them. The hardest thing to tell the parents are the emotional special needs. This isn't as concrete and it's harder to convince the parents.

We can identify the problem, we can make educated guesses, but we can't put a Band-Aid on it like a boo-boo. We can only be a stepping-stone to help the parents put it all in the right place.

Elementary School

Interview with an Elementary School Psychologist and an Elementary School Social Worker

What are some of the common questions you get from parents?

Mostly I get asked whether it's time to put the child into a private school rather than the public school. They are also concerned with who their contact person will be at the next level, whom they will be able to connect with, and who will be the guidance counselor and/or regular classroom teacher.

Do you have any threads that you have found make transitions work?

I think it's very important before the transition to have the new school meet the child's current teacher and meet the child. It's important to meet as a team and think about the needs of each child. Once again, giving parents a contact makes the transition go smoother. If they know who they can depend on at the next level, they feel a sense of connection and not so isolated. Trying to lock in a specific counselor ahead of time is crucial in certain specific cases. Selecting what you hope will be the appropriate counselor for the special needs child is essential. Doing as much as possible to familiarize the child and the parents at the next level leaves little room for surprises, and this makes everything go smoother.

One thing that helps avoid these surprises is to make sure that your child has an opportunity to visit the school on his own in addition to the visit with the whole class. For some children, it works better to have this individualized visit prior to the class visit. This makes it less overwhelming when they go with the class, and they have some idea what to expect at the next visit. Other children may prefer visiting on their own after the class visit, because now they have a clear idea of what they want to know about and what they want to focus on. Changes are especially hard for special needs children, because they are vulnerable and we ask different things of them than we do of the other kids. They are the ones that have the most difficulty with transition, because they are dealing with issues of separation, acceptance, and rejection. They are dealing with what is most difficult for any child, compounded by their special needs issues.

What are some of the major differences you see going from elementary school to middle school?

Old settings, especially in the elementary years, tend to be much more supportive and nurturing. In middle school, that same nurturing doesn't continue. Some things that helped them grow are now being taken away from them. Some children may not need the nurturing as much as others, but it still can be a difficult transition.

What's the most difficult for the parents?

Without a doubt, letting go. This and when the child enters kindergarten are two of the most difficult times along the twelve years. The parent feels less connected and more isolated. Support groups for parents of special needs children are a wonderful resource to help feel less isolated and more connected. It is sometimes harder for the parents to deal with the transition, because they are more aware of the impending changes that will be taking place. Based on experience, they can see the whole picture from a better vantage point, and this can sometimes cause concern. Also, when a child transitions to a new environment, he may be going over to the new environment with classmates. What can be a very positive feeling for the child in relating to school through his peers can be a very threatening feeling for the parent who is used to playing a more active role with the child—an "empty nest" syndrome. Entering middle school is a further step in the letting-go process as the child begins to move away from the parent and connects more with peers and teachers on his own. Parents usually feel they are going through this transition alone.

How much connection is there between the sending school and the receiving school?

As much as possible. It is important for both schools to be in touch with one another. That's our key role in transitioning the child from here, to put them in touch with the right people at the next level. When the system fails to carefully plan transition patterns, this can make it more difficult for parents and children.

How far in advance do you start preparing them?

The year before they go is enough. We find that the parents and the child are not really ready to deal with it any earlier than this. These children are struggling with the day-to-day issues; it's much too hard and irrelevant for some parents and special needs children to deal with a long-term issue until the year before. Timing of the preparation is important; if it is done too soon or even too late, it won't work. For parents, it is a matter of priorities. Sometimes they have other priorities that do not allow them to focus on the issues of transition too far in advance. Different people respond differently. Some people like to be prepared ahead of time, while others like to wait until the reality of the situation is closer at hand. We also need to look at the issues of the child and what they are coping with. This can also play into the decision of the timing of the preparation.

What are some specific issues during transition for a child who has special needs?

For some children, it may be the realization that they need to go to a different school or even out of district within the same town or city in order to receive the special services that they need. This can be a critical time, for students may feel depressed or may be reluctant to go. It can also be very hard for parents. Often both children and parents are receiving a mixed message in terms of the concept of mainstreaming. On the one hand, you are talking about mainstreaming students, yet because of where the services are located, you actually separate the child from the other students. It can be perceived by both parent and child as another type of rejection. Every transition is a rejection as well as a change, and that's why it is so hard for these students to deal with transitions. There's often a feeling that they have been bumped around and this is just another bump. Many people have "no idea how it feels to always feel different."

The counselors may need to have meetings with the parents on a regular basis to help prepare them for this particular type of transition.

What about the children's most common questions?

There really aren't typical questions that are asked. We feel that the special needs child is assured more than the other children in the process of transition. The learning disability teacher or the counselors tend to make lots of connections for these children. They help these children not be as worried because of this preparation. This is a more built-in preparation.

Secondary Education

The following is a group interview conducted with three members of the guidance department of a middle school: a learning center director, a guidance counselor/chairperson, and a department head guidance counselor.

What do you see as some of the most important steps in transitioning to high school?

An important step for transitioning from the elementary to the secondary level is to have a representative accompany the special needs family and consult at the feeder schools. They need to find out the needs of the students and how those needs will be addressed. It is also important for parents to initiate a meeting with the new school. They should come early to see the program and familiarize themselves with the school. That first contact is very important, because the parents have lots of fears and concerns, and this allows them to start dialoguing with the school.

This is a time when children are blossoming into adolescence, and that is a whole process in and of itself, and then when you couple this with the added dimension of the special needs and how they will transition into adolescence, different issues arise. What has happened to the child during the middle school years is crucial; parents need to recognize that a child may be very attached to a guidance counselor and teacher.

When do you start preparing the child for the transition?

Anxiety about high school and what they are going to experience really does not come until the year before the transition. This is another area in which the counselors are of great help. This anxiety can be about either achievement, for example, how hard the work will be, or social, worrying about who they will sit with at lunch, or both. As counselors, we need to validate these issues as they arise. We also need to reach out to the special needs students to start preparing them, for they rarely take the initiative to pursue the transition preparation, mainly because they aren't even aware of it. One of the ways we help them is to prepare them as much as possible to advocate for themselves, for the more they can own their own accountability and fine-tune their communication skills, the better prepared they will be. From this stage on, children usually want less parental involvement and want to advocate for themselves, using appropriate adults in the school.

What can parents do to help facilitate this advocacy level?

Sometimes, students can't hear the message from the parents but will hear it from a counselor. In other words, the parents may need to communicate to the counselor some of the issues their child is struggling with and ask the counselor to assist the child in resolving the issues, in learning how to access help for him or herself, and in learning to understand how to "work the system." Sometimes parents may be misguided or get the wrong information, so open lines of communication are essential. Good communication between the school and home is crucial. We run the gamut in the type of parents we deal with, from the too-concerned parents, who actually enable their child to be weaker, to the parents who don't even show up for the meetings and to whom we end up sending registered letters. One way in which counselors can assist the too-concerned parents is by being available to meet and reassure parents and by guiding parents to their own issues. Parents need to separate just whose issue they are dealing with, theirs or the child's. A parent who is very concerned can help the child by guiding the child rather than doing it for him. It is critical for counselors to take into consideration the psychodynamics of the family. Parents need to understand that there is a change in the relationship with the child.

Like other children, special needs children don't want to be different, and consequently, they may resist some of the supports that the parents want to put in place for them. Always remember to ask your children open-ended questions that lead to dialogue rather than closed questions. I truly believe that no child wants to do badly in school, but children develop behaviors that cover their shame when they don't do well. Kids need to work. No parent wants his child to be frustrated. Some students have lost the pleasure of pushing through frustration and reaping the benefit of satisfaction that comes from hard work. Are we stopping special needs students too soon?

Besides preparing the child academically, what other steps are in the process?

It is very important for the home and the school to come together as a team, through communicating and supporting the child. High school is a harder adjustment, both academically and socially. Homework becomes more of an issue. In middle school, there is a lot of nurturing, but the high school does not operate this way. The academic ante goes up, the homework increases, and there is less leeway in deadlines. The social ante also goes up. The social life in the middle school is more in transition and more dramatic, but the social risks in high school are higher. Social life in general for the special needs child can be difficult, at any level. It can be a major issue.

The special needs child can experience isolation, which can be very problematic in the middle schools. A lot of kids may experience a lot of rejection at this level. School can help eradicate some of this isolation, as a special needs student can get absorbed into the school on a day-to-day basis. It is important that special needs children have sufficient experiences in activities that are not academic, for example group activities like band, chorus, drama, and sports. They can foster friendships that can help the social experiences of the child. To parents, the best advice is to be pragmatic, not to personalize it, and to understand it is the child. In other words, try not to make a bigger issue than necessary. Also, to be realistic and understand your child's limitations. It does not mean that you don't have high expectations, but without realistic understanding, the parent can become angry if the child is not delivering or living up to expectations.

One way a parent can help a child prepare for a course is to be aware of the upcoming curriculum and do family-oriented activities to ready them. For example, if you know the child will be studying the 1950s, then going to see a film about the fifties might make the child have a better understanding of that decade before entering that class. A parent should be tuned in to what the child will be studying, for the more exposed a child can be, the better prepared he is to participate in class discussions and activities. It might be as simple as the teacher asking "Has anyone any idea what the fifties was like?" and this child can raise his hand and cite the movie, thus feeling confident and boosting self-esteem. It also makes other children take notice of this child.

It is important to share with the school any personal family history or current events that may influence the child in the school. This completes the loop so that the school can better understand and help the child. Kids need respect for their boundaries and we need to show them respect. Realize that children don't want to fail. Ask what the school can do to support what the child needs and how to sensitize the environment as to what the child needs.

What do you do next?

We meet as a team to evaluate the child. We call the parents and share our observances with them.

Interview with a High School Guidance Counselor

What are some common needs for parents?

They need help in knowing what's out there, how to find it, and then how to interpret what they find. They also find out that there are a million variations of the same thing, for example, there are colleges that are focused solely on special needs and then there are schools where the special needs departments are just one component of the school services.

What are some common needs of the students?

Basically they are the same as the parents. They hear the word "college," and they have difficulty understanding it from the general to the specific.

What is the biggest fear of the student?

"I'm not going to go anywhere" and "Will they want me?" are two of the biggest fears that I hear. Students don't seem as concerned with what the school will be like once they get there as much as the anxiety about being wanted by the school. Rejections are taken as a personal thing. Because they have a handicap, they assume that something is wrong with them and have a harder time accepting rejection and automatically assume that the rejection is based on the handicap.

I bet that last concern is a very common one.

It certainly is. And then I find out that a lot of the parents don't want the colleges to know that their child has a learning disability. Consequently, I spend time talking to parents. Parents have the feeling that telling a school about the child's learning disability will diminish the chances of being accepted. From my experience, it doesn't seem to be true, and I assure parents of this.

Is that the only concern?

No, another big concern is the myth that these students believe that there is only one school for them. They are looking for the school, and I assure them that there is more than one program and that they will have choices. I tell them not to be limited by their disability, that they are bigger than one school. I then assist them to identify all these different places.

Is being accepted by a college their only worry?

Basically yes. The other most commonly asked questions are more of a nuts-and-bolts nature. They ask, "How do I get information?" "When should I be doing this?" "Will you look at my essay?" "What is class rank?" "How do I get my transcript?" "How do I do research?"

How do you assist the parents?

One of the biggest tasks that I face with the parents is to assist them in separating their needs from the child's needs. Some parents do too much for their children, for example, they take it upon themselves to send away for the applications. The kids start thinking that they are not capable of even doing that themselves. I have to tell parents that they've already been to college and now it's the child's turn. Parents also need assurance. They are scared. They have fought battles for and with their children that other children haven't had. They need to know that it's okay to advocate for the child and they need the encouragement to do so. I also let the parents know that it is okay. We are both on the same wavelength, we are both on the same page in wanting to help get the kids ready to go out.

Does the issue of a special needs child taking a year off ever come up?

Lots. There are many programs that are available for students who aren't necessarily ready to go to college. And there are many children that would greatly benefit from postponing college. What I usually run up against is the fear of the parent that if the child takes a year off, the child will "never go back." I find just the opposite to be true. Kids do in fact go back, and in so many cases there were kids that would have been better off not going straight to college. The kids themselves will express the concern that they are not ready, and sometimes parents have a hard time listening to the kid. I end up helping the child to negotiate with the parent.

What is your role in assisting children with transition?

I try to get kids on the right time frame. They come in and bite their nails, and I say, "When it's time to worry, I'll let you know." I tell them to live in the present and don't be stressed out. I want them to see high school as more than a stepping-stone to the future. That's the hardest part of my job. There are things that naturally cause anxiety, like the PSAT. For the learning disabled, test anxiety prevails. They take an emotional beating on standardized testing, and I try to work with the kids. I tell them not to fall into the rut of comparing themselves to their peers. "You'll always lose." They lose sight of their own strengths. I help them look at their own strengths and define their uniqueness. I tell them that they all have something special to offer. I tell them to walk through the process, and that I will walk through it with them. I assure them that they are not isolated.

What other areas do you assist in transitioning?

I actually can be of help before the child even gets to high school. I will even meet a child before they enter high school. I'll have an eighth grader spend a day in the high school. There are two key rooms that I will make sure they know about before they come to high school. One is the guidance counselor's room and the other is the nurse's room. This plays a big part in helping to reduce the anxiety level. It's very important for the child to know that there is someone in the school that they can depend on and go to when they need assistance or reassurance. We have to keep in mind that they are dealing with normal adolescent issues as well as their special needs issues.

What about when the student first arrives?

I will accompany the students to class. I will set small goals for them, have them take small steps, so as not to overwhelm them. I individualize for each child and I am flexible to their needs. It's really important to "go that extra mile." The best reassurance I can offer a child is to let them know that they are my first priority. I'm their advocate. I want their parents involved, but they come first.

As we mentioned earlier, transitioning is an ongoing process and it does not end up with formal education. For some children with special needs, independent living may be an important issue. For these situations, we include an interview on guardianship.

Interview with a Lawyer for Guardianship

What exactly do you do as a guardianship lawyer?

My job is actually twofold. First, I oversee and coordinate the entire guardianship process. My other job is to actually educate the parent.

Educate the parent?

You'd be surprised how much information needs to be imparted to the parent. Guardianship can involve a lot of deprivation of rights to the potential candidate. I truly believe it's actually a little overrestrictive. For example, a ward. . . .

Excuse me for interrupting, but what is a ward?

A ward is what we call the individual once he or she has been placed under guardianship. The ward is deprived of some other rights, like not being able to make and/or sign contracts, choose where to live, and choose to travel, just to name a few examples. Obviously, for the severely impaired individual, these are not necessarily negative factors, but for the individual that's not so severe, the more mildly impaired, this could be a real detriment. And this could be an issue. Different states have different guidelines for determining guardianship, but the bottom line here is that the individual has to be declared incompetent to some degree to be eligible for guardianship, and that's a hard concept to swallow. These are some of the negatives.

What about the positives? Actually, let's go back. How about defining exactly what a guardian is.

The guardian is the person legally appointed to make decisions for another person. The relationship between the guardian and a ward is called a fiduciary relationship. This means that one person is legally entrusted to care for another person.

Okay, now the positives.

I think the most prevalent is protection. This way, the impaired person can't be taken advantage of with any financial scams, and also medical decisions that need to be made are made by the guardian. Since the individual may not be able to make a good medical decision, the guardian can do so. In fact, a lot of hospitals are reluctant to do intrusive treatment or surgery on individuals with impairments who do not have guardians. This makes them more susceptible to getting sued, because if something goes wrong, they can be sued and questioned why they allowed someone who wasn't capable of making a decision to sign legal papers concerning their medical treatment. If the individual has a guardian, the hospitals are covered. It is not a definite rule, but it makes the hospitals feel safer.

So, a guardian protects all this?

Well, not everything. There are certain issues that a guardian can't do or make decisions about without always first going to court. Guardians do not have authority over intrusive or controversial issues. Some of the issues covered here include if the ward wants to have an abortion or if anyone wants to perform sterilization or experimental or intrusive medical treatment. Also, this includes the use of antipsychotic drugs. The guardian has to go back to court for each of these kinds of issues so that the guardian is not the sole decision maker.

Is the guardian always the parent?

Not always. If the parent is dying or ill or feels that he or she won't be able to take care of the individual in any capacity, then someone else will be the guardian.

Let's go back to the comment you made about being overly restrictive. Is there any way around this?

There seems to be a new trend in guardianship called limited guardianship. This type of guardianship restricts a guardian's decision-making authority to a specific area, such as medical decisions. This way, the ward holds on to rights in other areas, such as choosing where to live. Temporary guardianship might be appropriate for short-term emergencies. You can ask a lawyer about other legal ways to protect a person with a disability that aren't as restrictive as guardianship. These could include such areas as healthcare proxies, trusts, and representative payee.

That sounds so much better than all the restrictions you said earlier.

Right. Even for a limited guardianship, a ward has to be declared incompetent in at least one specific area. However, they do get to retain many of the rights they would have lost under full guardianship (where to live, contracts, travel, etc.).

How does this guardianship process affect benefits from special education?

Guardianship doesn't affect anything dealing with special education. All the services stay intact whether the person is under legal guardianship or not.

How do you put guardianship into place? What are the steps you take?

The first thing that has to be done is initiate a clinical team to evaluate the individual. This would include a psychologist, a social worker, and a physician. If the team doesn't feel that the individual needs guardianship, it's pretty much a done deal. If the team thinks that the individual requires guardianship, then it files an evaluation report with the court and a petition. The petition is basically a formal request for the person who is seeking guardianship. The guardian has to file a bond form with the court. This is a promise to the court to fulfill the statutory duties. The guardian is liable if he doesn't act in the ward's best interest.

Does the person seeking guardianship always have to use a lawyer?

Not necessarily, but I do recommend it. There is a lot to coordinate and a lot of time deadlines. A lawyer can really help with all this.

What happens after the person is granted guardianship? Is that the end of it?

In most states, there is a requirement for an annual report from the guardian, something they have to file. Remember, different states have varying requirements for seeking guardianship. The best thing for a person to do if he is seeking guardianship for an individual is to call the state department for the particular problem, such as the Department of Mental Health, and request information for guardianship.

Summary

Maria: As the time approached for my child to move from elementary school to middle school, I started wondering and worrying about a number of things:

- How would my child handle going to a bigger school?
- How well would my child do dealing with various teachers (as opposed to having one main teacher), changes in schedules, and long-term assignments?
- How could I help my child recognize her concerns with leaving and her fears about the new school?

Should I wait for her to raise the issue, or should I bring it up?

- How helpful and accommodating would the new school be?
- How long would it take them to get to know and care for my child?
- Who would be my contact person?
- How could I communicate the struggles and gains of the past few years, so they could understand and appreciate her fully and they could understand my concerns, within the context of our reality?
- How soon do I need to actively involve myself with the new school?

I started dealing with my anxiety by realizing and accepting that transitioning to a new environment required work and though many things were out of my control, there were some steps that I could initiate and be directly involved with. Once again, I had to be proactive and prepare myself and my child for the move.

Sandy: My biggest fear of transitioning from elementary school to middle school for my child definitely was in the physical realm. My daughter's physical limitations are mild and she is mobile, but the limitations are impeding enough to make certain tasks more difficult, so my concerns were varied. How will she walk around the school? How will she change classes? How will she enter the school? How will this affect her socially? Will she be tired walking around the school? How will she change for gym? How will she open her locker? How will she carry her book bag? These concerns were so overwhelming, I almost overlooked the academic issues.

Parents take a jolt. If a child transitions successfully at one level, they might assume that the child is an easy transitioner for any situation. It is important to look for any signs that a child may be having difficulty transitioning. If you notice any changes in behavior—for example, changes in sleeping and eating patterns or energy level, or mood swings—the child could be signaling that he is having difficulties in transitions. It could be signaling anything that is going on in the child's life, but it is important for the parent to look at the whole picture of what is happening in the world of the child. That is to say, if different behavior patterns do emerge, it's important that the parent not overlook the possibility that it can be traced to transitioning. Children have a difficult time expressing stress or pinpointing its source, and we as parents must look everywhere for the source, including the possibility that it might mean some transitioning difficulties.

Some steps to take to prepare yourself for a transition are the following:

1. Visit the new school, without the child, and meet the principal and guidance counselor. Familiarize yourself with the curriculum, support services, special education programs, even the layout of the building. Visit some of the classes and observe. This allows you to have realistic expectations of what will be available. You will also have some concrete and factual information that you can share with your child.

2. At a later date, schedule a visit for your child. Though many schools schedule a day for the whole class to come for a visit, a child with special needs will benefit from having a visit on his own, preferably before the class visit takes place. When the child visits independently, he can receive more individual attention and the visit can be paced more appropriately to meet the needs of the child. When your child visits the new school with his classmates, he will have an idea of what to expect and the visit will not seem so chaotic, thus hopefully preventing your child from feeling overwhelmed and anxious at the end of the visit.

3. Call the school your child is presently attending and ask them about their procedure for transitioning students to new schools or programs. How do they do it? When do they do it? Is there a scheduled meeting and who attends? How much time is allotted at these meetings? What information will be shared?

4. If your child receives any services outside the school system, contact them and request some input from their perspective. (How is your child doing presently? What kind of help/support do they feel your child will need in the new environment? What would they like you to communicate to the transition team and the new school about your child?) This information will help you in preparing yourself to present information that accurately describes your child's needs, and/or help you refute (with documentation and backup) information that is inaccurate or outdated. By asking for input from others who know and work with your child, you will feel better prepared and more confident in asking and negotiating in your child's best interest.

5. During a transition meeting, it might be beneficial to bring an advocate or a friend with you. This person can assist you during the meeting to convey your ideas or information more clearly. After the meeting, the advocate can help you clarify what transpired during the meeting and what may be some areas that need further follow-up.

6. If, after the transition meeting ends, you feel that not all of the pertinent issues and information have been addressed, be assertive in stating that the allotted time has been insufficient and negotiate on a follow-up meeting within an acceptable time frame.

7. If you feel satisfied with the transition meeting but feel that the new school staff needs some more in-depth information prior to making decisions regarding teacher and counselor assignment, schedule an immediate follow-up meeting with the new school. Explain that there are issues, concerns, or information that need to be taken into account because of the new setting and that should be discussed privately rather than in an open meeting.

8. Try to identify a few parents in your community that have recently gone through the transition you are facing with their special needs child. Once again, networking with other parents is a marvelous opportunity to gather invaluable information. Through them you can familiarize yourself with the strengths and weaknesses of a new environment or program, picking up some tips that might help your child socially or academically or hearing of difficulties they might have encountered and how they approached the issue and resolved it. The more familiar you are with a new environment and the more you understand about protocol and how to access information and help, the more likely you are to attain positive gains for your child.

An important factor to note is the time frame of transitioning. Sometimes a child might be well adjusted or seem well adjusted to a new setting for a few weeks, then when the new dust settles and the new routines take shape, the child may experience difficulty. This is a delayed reaction to the new environment. The possibility that the child's problems may be related to transitioning cannot be dismissed and must be addressed. That the problems the child is experiencing are related to transitions may elude us, because we are holding on to the initial positive response that we so anxiously seek at the beginning of a new setting.

It's important to encourage the child to speak up, share feelings, and ask questions about the impending change. We need to elicit information from our children by asking, "What would you like to know?" "Talk to me." They may have a difficult time pinpointing what is causing them anxiety, but by engaging them in a conversation, we can be instrumental in assisting them to uncover the source of their concern. The child may not even realize the source of his anxiety, but by engaging in a verbal dialogue, he can suddenly realize just what is bothering him. What seems like an overwhelming feeling of anxiety about a large sea of unknown might in reality only be one specific area of concern.

For example, a young child may be looking ahead at a new school with much anxiety about the whole process. But when he actually verbalizes the feeling, he may realize that it is only one piece of the picture that is disturbing him, such as being afraid to get on the school bus. All along, he may have thought it was the entire picture, when in reality, he has no concerns about the actual school, new teachers, new friends, schoolwork, etc., but rather just the means by which he gets there. By pinpointing this area, both you and your child can address that one issue, work it out, and thus make the transition process a smoother one. In some cases, it may be more than one area, or the area may not be so easily defined, but in any case, this step-by-step process can lead to a smoother transition.

Some other possible questions that may help the child are: "What do you want me to do?" "How can I help you?" "What are you expecting and what do you think is going to happen?" Along those lines, we have to acknowledge that we as parents are not the sole influence in their lives. Through peers, the media, and other external influences, the child acquires information about life. For example, a young neighbor a few grades ahead of him may give him information about a teacher in the school that frightens the child. It may be based on hearsay, a personal isolated experience, or just childhood exaggeration. The child may be internalizing this and may not be aware that we as parents can help him with this. By dialoguing with some of the above questions, we learn of the child's anxiety and then help him deal with it. We're not always aware of these other variables. We may assume that the child's anxieties are based on their special needs and might discover that it isn't always related to the specific special needs.

Transitioning doesn't confine itself from school to school. It also includes grade to grade, school to vacation, vacation to school, school to summer, summer to school, any situation that alters the child's routine. For some, it can even be class to class. For some children, it can be as extreme as from the home environment to the school environment on a daily basis. A child with a physical disability, for instance, can have a hard time transitioning from the physical layout of the home to the school environment. These are not always constant. They may fluctuate greatly, and the children may even experience lapses. Awareness by parents is a key factor especially in teaching the child some coping mechanisms to deal with the transitions. It might not eliminate the core of the problem, but rather help the child deal with it more successfully. Like so many other areas in the life of the special needs child, we want to provide the independent skills to deal with life's experiences and demands, and transitioning is one more step along the way.

In general, life is one large transition, from stage to stage, school to school, age to age, minute to minute. While no one can predict the next moment and our future, we all must do our best to be as prepared as possible, to know our strengths and weaknesses, and then we can be better able to handle whatever life wants us to be ready for.

8

Support Systems

Inherent in having a special needs child is the necessity for a support system. The term *support system* can cover as narrow a range as a friend to turn to when you need someone to talk to, to a wider range of professionals. In talking about support systems, we are not limiting the focus to those services needed to help the child with special needs. The parent(s), the sibling(s), and the whole family may need to consider them as well. You might wonder how a parent seeking help for himself or herself is going to help the child. That question and the question of how to best help your child with a support system will both be answered in this chapter. Let's start with the child.

Support Systems for the Child

Putting a support system into place for your child is another branch on the tree of life, another avenue that must be traveled to offer the best help you can. Your child has been asked to travel this path in a different manner than anyone anticipated, and that path has many bumps and forks. Someone other than yourself should be there to guide the child. You the parent are your child's best advocate. But just as you rely on professional teachers to help educate your child and medical doctors to help treat your child, it is crucial that you turn to professionals for help in the psychology area.

Your children need to know that someone is available to hear their problems, to help in problem solving, to be good listeners, to be emotional healers, and a safe haven where they can share thoughts, emotions, fears, concerns, whatever, with someone other than the parent. The support person, in a sense, is also the central clearinghouse for all the emotional baggage, to deal with issues that don't quite fit in the teacher's area or the doctor's area. The type of help that is sought will obviously vary from child to child depending on the child's age, the availability, and the child's special needs. At best, the school psychologist, social worker, or school guidance counselor should be a definite support system. Outside the school, there are a wide variety of sources: social workers, psychologists, psychiatrists, organizations offering support, and so on. Also, don't overlook support systems such as religious groups and peer groups. Lots of schools have peer groups built into their programs that are offered to the special needs child.

No matter where you are seeking the information and help, make sure it is what you need and follow up on its success rate. It is very easy to slip into a pattern and not be aware if the support system is functioning or is being efficient and helpful. If your child is seeking advice from the school, whether through a peer group or guidance counselor, talk to the leader; make an appointment and keep abreast of what is going on. That is not to break the lines of confidentiality between your child and the support system, but rather to make sure it is functioning in a positive way for your child. Ask your child questions to make sure that this is the right source for him. It is imperative at this point to discuss the confidentiality issue. Make it clear to your child that your appointment with the counselor is not to impede on confidentiality, but to make sure that all is running smoothly.

Our daughters were in a peer group in which confidentiality was stressed each time they met; how important it was to be able to know that what was said within the confines of the room would go no further. As parents, we must respect that and not pry into our children's private issues if they need to confide in an outside source. The child must know that he can discuss anything and that it will stay with that person. This is especially true as children get older and there are issues they don't feel comfortable discussing with the parents.

Respecting confidentiality doesn't preclude our earlier suggestion of follow-up visits with the support person; we're just emphasizing the need to understand confidentiality. Of course, there is a fine line between what transpires in confidence between the child and therapist and what the parent should be told. For example, if the child is frustrated at something that the parent is doing, the child must feel safe that he can share this with his therapist and "complain" about his mother or father or both, and try to work it out through the therapist, if that is the route that the child wants to follow. If the therapist feels that it would be in the best interest of the child to discuss this issue with the parent, then the therapist will lead the child in that direction. Sometimes family counseling is an alternative or

addition to individual counseling. After all, the special
needs child has special siblings and special parents.

Using Support Systems

As your child encounters problems or runs into difficulties,
this becomes the time for you to make connections for him
regarding the different support systems he may have available and to steer him into accessing them. In this manner,
you are helping your child gain independence—you teach
him to recognize his support systems and learn when and
how to activate them. And you learn to share some of the
tasks of raising and educating a child with special needs
with other professionals.

This last point is very important, because as parents you
often have to wear many different hats and you may often
feel that you have to do everything. At times, some of the
ongoing involvement and support required by your children puts you at odds with them, creates tension and friction as you struggle to remain on top of necessary tasks
and information. Thus, it is necessary to sometimes have
that involvement with other professionals in the field. This
does not mean that you are out of the picture or out of the
loop. On the contrary, you are in touch with these support
systems, and you can provide input, gain insight from their
perspectives, and continue to have a clear vision of the big
picture that surrounds your child's life.

Let's return to the importance of teaching your child to
recognize his support systems and to learn to activate
them. You should understand clearly what these support
systems can do and be willing to develop a team relationship with them. In other words, as a team, you are all
needed, and the skills and knowledge of everyone should

be tapped. Some ways to steer your child in using his support system might be the following:

- If he is having difficulty with an assignment or project, you could say, "That is something you should discuss with your teacher or with your tutor."
- If he is in middle school and is having difficulties with a teacher or with peers, you could say, "I think you should meet with your counselor about this to discuss ways in which you can solve this issue." At times, it might be necessary for you to touch base with the counselor before and/or after your child is to meet with the counselor, but that needs to be decided by you based on your child's needs, age, and the issue at hand.
- If your child is seeing a counselor, psychologist, or psychiatrist, it might be helpful for the child if you point out things that might be good to share in the sessions. For example, if your child is feeling very upset or disappointed about a recent experience, even though he has shared his feelings with you, you can say, "That might be something you want to share with your therapist when you meet with him."

In these suggestions, it might appear that you are stepping away from your child and not being the integral part of his life that both of you are so accustomed to. It is important to make clear to your child that you are not neglecting his concerns and that you are always there and available to help him, but it is good to get other advice and other strategies for solving the problem.

When your child is younger, it is often necessary for you to become the intermediary between your child and the outside world. Depending on your child's special needs and abilities, as he gets older, you need to shift gears and direct your child to access supports and negotiate situations for himself, in order to gain experience and confidence in becoming his own advocate. It is very difficult at times to see him struggling and not intervene, but if you are to really help him, you may need to hold back and permit him to struggle.

Multiple Support Systems

In seeking support systems, it is crucial to have more than one source. The following is actually gathered from an unfortunate situation that took place in the course of writing this book.

Sandy: My daughter Rayna fortunately had many support systems in place, and thanks to this wide range of support systems, the trauma that happened to her followed a smoother path, in her seeking help and getting through the trauma. She had been seeing a wonderful psychologist, Dr. Gardner, since the age of six for seven years of her life—more than half of her life. They shared a wonderful relationship, and the therapist "lived" through a lot of my daughter's medical turmoil, experiencing her ups and downs in her medical stability. The therapist was a warm and compassionate person, a true emotional healer for my daughter as well as a special friend to her. Rayna always looked forward to her visits with her therapist.

While we were writing this book, the therapist died suddenly of an aneurysm, at the age of fifty-one. The impact of her death on my daughter was devastating. This woman had been an integral part of my daughter's life, a true support system, an emotional healer, and a friend. Losing her is a void that will linger for a long time, not just for my daughter but for me as well. Her death taught me many things, and I move on in life with her teachings as a legacy. She taught me about life, how precious it is, how vulnerable we are to its existence, and how each day is a very special gift.

The most important lesson in relationship to this book is the absolute, unequivocal necessity to make sure you have more than one support system in place and that you teach your child how and when to access them or activate them. That doesn't necessarily mean juggling two therapists, but rather to have other people your child can talk to, other people who know your child, so that your child is able to seek out other sources for help. Because Rayna was so familiar with the school guidance counselor and had been in a recent support group for peers, she immediately had other sources to turn to for help in this grieving process. She also sought out our religious leader, also a true source for comfort.

It would have been much more difficult for Rayna if she had to see a therapist or a professional who didn't already know Rayna and her background. Rayna was able to immediately turn to her sources and jump into how hard it was for her to deal with this death. She didn't have to start explaining her history of her medical condition and why she was seeing this therapist or any background information. The people she sought out were quickly able to help her deal with the grieving. They were people Rayna knew well and was very comfortable with. We were able to make the transition to a new therapist gradually, using these wonderful people as stepping-stones to bridge the gap between the therapist that died and a new "replacement."

Of course, there will never be a replacement, just a new person to help Rayna with her special needs.

The death of Dr. Gardner is a rare example of losing a support system, a scenario that is seldom rather than often but nevertheless does exist and did happen. Other possibilities of losing therapists exist: they may retire or move away, for example. These cases involve a loss in another way, yet there is preparation time for the transition. New support systems can be put in place by working with both the old and the new therapist, although there are difficulties here, too. If, for example, a therapist announces that he is moving away, the child may have feelings about this news that he might find difficult sharing with the therapist. He may feel anger or fear and not want to discuss this with the therapist. Again, having other support systems in place can be most helpful.

Support Systems for the Parent

In discussing support systems, it is important to keep in mind that seeking out support as an adult is an indirect way of helping your special needs child. We have been encouraging you, the parent, to learn how to advocate, to network, to organize, to be strong, to have courage—do this, that, and everything. That can be a very tough juggling act. You, too, need some support. Fear or misconceptions of what support groups or counseling sessions entail keep many from seeking and participating in a source of comfort, insight, and understanding, to identify strategies that can enhance the quality of daily living. For some people, seeking help for themselves is a sign of weakness; others feel that they do not need someone to tell them what to do; still others may be afraid of being told that they are not good parents. Yet, as we spoke to parents whose children varied in age and in their special needs, one piece of wisdom surfaced over and over again: the value of a support system.

Seeking help is a sign of strength, for it takes courage to face your issues rather than deny them or downplay them. Telling you what to do is not the goal of a support system or counseling session. And seeking help is not an indication that you are a bad or inadequate parent but an indication that you want to learn and understand. By helping yourself, you are, in essence helping your special needs child. You need someone to be able to talk to, to share your concerns, fears, frustrations, hopes, and dreams.

One situation that seems to be prevalent among the parents we interviewed is the empty nest syndrome, but a step further. When we first learn about the child's diagnosis, whether it is at birth or several years down the road, we throw ourselves into the situation with a full-blown speed. We focus everything we have on dealing with it, whether it is the initial running around to confirm a diagnosis, obtaining second opinions, running here, there, and everywhere for tests, answers, cures, miracles. We put our energies to these external tasks, and sometimes, by denial or by sheer exhaustion, we don't look inward for our reactions, feelings, and our true fears. We don't digest what has happened and emotionally process the reality of the situation.

If you are constantly running around and making telephone calls, then you are dealing with the reality, but you don't have to face the reality. There is a big difference. Dealing with the reality can take the form of running around to doctors and teachers, making endless telephone calls, etc. Facing the reality is looking at your child, when the telephone is silent and the car sits in the driveway, and seeing what you are faced with. When the dust settles, and life falls into whatever routine it does (albeit some routines stay smoother, while other are constantly interrupted), you find yourself empty. The world can seem very quiet and very frightening. Hidden personal feelings may emerge and take over in a devastating way. This is the time when you have to deal with all that has occurred and live with the consequences of the reality. This can be very painful. A support system, if not already in place, is crucial at this time. Professional support is ideal, but parent support can also be an integral part of this process of facing the pain.

Realizing that this reaction is "normal" is just one step in being emotionally healthy when dealt such devastating news. No parent plans on a child that will have special needs. We all face our future with the hope that our offspring will be normal and healthy. Getting this jolt of unexpected news is devastating, and the more we can have support systems and rely on professionals to help us through, the better we are, and subsequently the more enabled we are to best help our special needs child.

9

Special Siblings, Special Parents

During the course of our interviews on transitions (see Chapter 7), we came to the realization that both of us enjoyed gathering information, but what we savored most was the unique way in which each interviewee expressed his or her own thoughts. As we asked questions, it was very interesting to see how different aspects of similar questions were given more importance or emphasis, based on the individual's experience and present reality.

We could easily summarize the main concepts or facts that we have come across or paraphrase what others have shared with us, but that would mainly provide you with our interpretation of the dialogues that transpired. Providing our readers with an opportunity to listen to other voices seems more valuable and enriching.

Thus, in the following pages, we share with you the thoughts and voices of other parents. Maybe, like us, you will be prompted by these interviews to reflect and put things in perspective, to identify with others and to share, making you more aware of facts you had never contemplated or had considered in isolation.

We have tried to present special needs in as universal a fashion as possible. This includes talking about special parents and special siblings. We understand that the dynamics of each family are not going to be the same; while some facets are universal, there are also some wide and diverse components to the family unit. There are the traditional units of the mother and father; there is the single-parent family, whether that parent is the mother or father or a surrogate parent. There are also differences in socioeconomic factors. These differences do not preclude effectiveness, nor do they mandate not being the ultimate advocate.

Life experiences might not flow as easily for some as they do for others. The home environment for each child will not be the same, nor will each school situation. Support systems may vary with the makeup of the family, such as support from grandparents, siblings, extended relatives, etc. We have endeavored to present as many diverse situations as possible. In our interviews, you will meet families with a single parent, two parents, a single child, siblings, a single special needs child, and more than one special needs child. We are just two parents with special needs children, and we want to include in our book different voices and diverse experiences.

We are dealing with more than just a special needs child. There is the special parent, the special sibling, the special friend, and the special family as a whole. There are significant others in the life of the child with special needs who will play an important role in helping the child cope and face his difficulties, who will be influential in the child's development of self-esteem, confidence, and outlook on life. We need to remember that these significant others will in turn be touched by their interactions and experiences with a special needs child. How do the siblings feel? How do the friends and the grandparents feel?

As you read these interviews, you may find aspects that you can relate to or from which you can extrapolate what is relevant to your situation. Use these interviews as a support system in print that might help you understand and know that you are not alone in this journey and experience. When you do connect with others—find a support group, or meet other parents of children with special needs—ask some of the questions we have asked in the interviews and share some of the answers you have found in these chapters. As you speak and share, you will find that many parents are very willing to share information and assist you in locating resources. You will really see that you are indeed not alone and that through your connections and networking you can eliminate or alleviate your sense of isolation.

The Interviews

For the first two interviews, we selected one parent who had just found out that her five-year-old has special needs, and the other parent who had "been at it" for a long time. You can see two very different parents, Laura and Ann, at completely opposite ends of the spectrum. Of course, there are thousands of scenarios in between, the child born with special needs, the senior in high school who is suddenly diagnosed with a learning problem, the fifth grader, the second grader, the college student. Both medically and educationally, anything can change at any time.

Interview with Laura, Mother of a
Five-Year-Old Learning Disabled Child

When did you find out your child has learning problems?

A few weeks ago. The teacher called me to tell me that she was seeing signs of reading problems. So we decided to test her and found out she had some language-based problems, word retrieval issues, and processing of information.

May I ask how all this affected you?

I was shocked. There had been no signs, because she just started kindergarten and nothing stood out as any red flags that my child wasn't on target. But as she got into school more, her teacher started noticing little things. I'm still denying that she has to go to special teachers and have a special program. The first time I went to an IEP meeting, I was so overwhelmed.

How so?

Well, I sat down, and it was so official feeling, like being in a courtroom, and so legal that I had to sign my name to a paper! It was a scary feeling to be talking about my child in front of all these people. It was even weirder to hear all these people taking about my child. At one point, I thought I was going to cry. I wish I had brought my husband or a friend. I wish I had known more about it, read some books, asked some friends, even asked the teachers more. I mean, they were very informative, telling me exactly what they were going to accomplish and who would be there, and so forth. But, it's one thing to hear that, and another thing to walk into the room and experience it. I wish I had asked another parent to tell me about it.

What else did you feel?

I was completely waiting during the whole meeting for them to say, well, we made a mistake or based on our tests she really is okay, but that never happened. I was scribbling things down that I wanted to remember on the side of one of the reports they handed me. I also didn't know what to do with half of the reports. Everyone was sweet and friendly and I really felt they had the best interest of my child in mind, but it was still upsetting. I actually asked the school guidance counselor to give me names of books to read and someone else who has a child with similar problems. She couldn't do that because of confidentiality, so I asked her to tell another parent to call me if she wanted to discuss things, and the next week I got a phone call from a mother who had a son in second grade. We met for coffee, and I felt like Dorothy returning to Kansas. It was so reassuring to meet someone else. I've met a few others, in fact one belongs to a group that meets at the high school, so the first parent I met and I are going together.

At what stage are you now?

Well, from those first few weeks of not being able to sleep to now feeling life isn't so bad—just a little different, but not so bad.

Interview with Ann, Mother of a High School Son
with ADD (Attention Deficit Disorder)

What has been the impact on the family and what strategies have you used to survive?

When I think of strategies it has been a lot easier because I have been in education and have access to a lot of literature. Reading is my way of learning. It is helpful to understand my child's disability. They have helped me understand the parameters for the disability both from a neurological perspective and as a parent.

Being in a support group, in a mothers' group, has been very helpful. The most important thing is to be active listeners to each other's problems. Our pain happened at different levels, for example, when we had to understand and accept our child's disability. Having friends who understand active listening, who do not go immediately to suggestions; having people who share information about local pediatricians or dentists who understand children with ADD; that kind of networking is what you get from a support group. It has enabled us not to lower our expectations of our children. Just because they can't do it the same way as other children do does not mean they can't learn. They can learn to do it differently. I have told my son that I will support him but that he cannot use his disability to get off the hook. Send the message: "You can do this. I won't let you off the hook. I will support you."

Going to see the therapist is another useful strategy. Before I understood his disability, I thought the child's difficulties were something I had done as a parent. First I saw a psychiatrist, but it was not the right fit. I did better with a psychologist who understood ADD. It can be helpful to view therapists as a support system that can provide parents and children with compensatory strategies.

It is also very important to be honest with your child. Point out when the disability gets in the way. Get him to understand himself, to know his own processing style. For example, point out to him that if he does not eat every two hours, he can't focus; if he does not sleep well, he can't focus; if he does not write his paper ahead of time, he will not have time to develop an outline, to review his work, and get any help he may need. I had to teach him that he cannot put the responsibility on the teacher. If it is a time management issue, there needs to be lead time. This should be written in the IEP.

We worked on a lot of organization skills before adolescence. We did charts that included the whole family, to show how we all used organization skills. It was built in as a family routine. Later it becomes more difficult to initiate. When your child is in elementary school, tell the teacher that you need to know when assignments and projects are going to be due, because this is how your family organizes itself. When your child reaches middle school or high school, this has become part of his routine and he will not be so apt to fight you on this.

As parents, we also need to remember that every year is a new conversation with teachers. This is a parent's reality. We need to keep on doing it when the child gets to middle school and changes classes and teachers every quarter or semester. Do it ahead of time. Set up a meeting, give a phone number where you can be reached, indicate that you will not tolerate that your child will be failed. It can feel burdensome at times, and you will ask, "When will it end?" College? Perhaps!

Other things that make a huge difference: to understand that children with any sort of disability do better if they can anticipate the shape of the day or the week. If the child is told very clearly what will happen that day, if you write it down and teach him to tell time, then the anxiety drops tremendously. These children tend to have a low tolerance for transitions. They need to know ahead of time if changes will take place. For example, you let him know that if you are going to be late to pick him up, the principal will receive a call from you, and the principal will then inform the child of the change. If you are sloppy about organization, you need to change for your child's sake. Read this book, it will help! Like many things in life, it can become a routine, and you just do it. There are times when I am tired and I am not good about giving my child notice, an indication that something is going to change, for example, to let him know that dinner will be served in five minutes, that we are leaving in ten minutes, etc. If I forget to warn him that dinner will be ready soon and call him to come down, I have learned that if he is doing written work, I need to give him time, I need to be flexible.

Food can be a real problem in a family if they have rigid expectations about eating times. A child may need to eat small meals every two hours, and he may need certain foods. It might be helpful to have a section in the kitchen where you stack certain snacks that your child can have. Indicate to your child that that is the place where he can go when he needs a snack between meals.

What things have been more difficult, and what has helped along the way?

When I meet a teacher who does not understand the need for compensatory strategies and states that it is not fair to the other kids in the class. I have learned that it is helpful to have some examples ready that will allow me to answer the question without being confrontational. For example, I will say to the teacher, "If a child could not see, would you deny him glasses? Would you refuse to accept having a child use a wheelchair? A hearing aid?"

What are some common needs for parents?

The need for information, the need for some sort of support. This comes in all shapes and forms. Also, it helps to be able to get information in videos and audiocassettes. People process information differently, and it's important to have a variety of media accessible to get the information. People could listen to some of the information to and from work in their car. Some excellent tapes are those by Richard Lavoie. He covers everything that has to do with learning disabilities, and the information is directed to teachers and parents.

When and how one hears information is important. There are times when I do a better job of processing. When I first got started, I was very overwhelmed. Over time, I learned that was a normal process, part of the learning process. The timing is very important. Keep this in mind when you try to share information about your child with teachers. Parents should prepare a handout of one or two pages to give to teachers. If it is longer, they will not read it.

When you are starting to learn about something, you need simple information. I see it as a Velcro surface. The more Velcro I have, the more I can absorb. I need to achieve the Velcro.

At times, I feel saturated and I do not want to read another thing. This tends to happen when my son is doing well, when things are running smoothly. I have learned to enjoy it while it lasts. What else is really a need is to have a knowledgeable listener, a support group or a therapist or both.

What has been your role in assisting other parents?

Sharing articles, names of good evaluators, experiences of things that have worked, names of doctors. I have given speeches, talked about advocating for learning disabled children. In my job as a curriculum specialist, I am constantly giving parents articles and titles of books. I see this as part of my job. I talk to them about homework and how to handle it. If the child is dealing with issues of distraction, I talk about how to set up a room that is monochromatic, how to monitor desk space (clear and clean), and if the child has posters in his bedroom, not to have them facing the child's work area.

Talk about issues regarding color. Some people are very color-sensitive, and some colors can zone out a child (the profusion of colors). We had a consultant come to our house and take a look at our son's room. She asked us, "Could you bear to live in this room?" I don't know why we think that children's rooms need to have bright colors and be very busy. We got bins and put toys inside the bins. We labeled each bin and taught our son that when he was done playing with one game, he needed to put it back in the bin, otherwise he would end up with all the toys on the floor and would not be able to focus on any of them.

Don't have a multicolored bedspread or striped sheets. Have the walls, bedspread, and rugs all in light colors.

Clutter also needs to be monitored. As the child gets older, there is a fine line between when to get involved and when to allow for independence. I repeat to my child something I heard a long time ago: there has to be a clear path that you can walk in your bedroom in case of a fire. When the clutter is such that I can't walk through, it is time to demand that things be picked up. I think I'm rambling.

No, that's okay. Even if some of what you say only applies to your child's particular special needs, there are still a lot of universal thoughts, such as cleaning up a room. It also points out how important it is to be on top of your child's disability. You have learned that colored sheets do not work for your child's disability; while this may not be an issue with other children's special needs, the bottom line is you know what the needs are and you have found out what to do about it.

Thanks, that's what it's all about, knowing your child's needs and trying to adapt to them and facilitate them.

What have you learned from this experience that has been the most valuable?

I have learned to listen and observe my child. I have also gotten such joy from his strengths. Ways of compensating have gotten to be such routines that they no longer take up most of my time. Moving from the child of our anxiety to the child of our pride—he is so giving. This summer he will work on a program to help children and to build houses for the elderly.

In the past, we have always focused on the problems. If we become knowledgeable and accepting, we can move to what we need to do as parents. We need to understand and take control of the situation without necessarily controlling the child. Understand what you need to do for the child, and know that this will also change over time. Parents need to be aware to back off; to learn to do advocacy silently, not in his face when the child gets older.

I have learned the importance of a support group. There are a lot of groups out there. People make a mistake not accessing this, because it validates their aloneness, their feelings of being the only parent with a struggling child.

It is important to help teachers understand that a child's public persona may be strong. While he is in school, he uses everything he has to keep it together, but when he comes home, he unravels. This is appropriate because home is where the child feels safe. There are kids who become unstuck in school. They might be dealing with a tough situation at home. This is a very different situation from the child that does not cause problems in school. How do you advocate for the child who in school seems to be doing well, but unravels at home? We need to tell teachers that we are a partnership, that we need their help. Bringing teachers into the loop of understanding is crucial. Teachers need to understand a child's behavior, that is part of the disability.

There is also a need for understanding social functions and social interactions. If a child does not have good social skills, this can be the most disabling component of his disability. A learning disabled child with social skills does ten times better than one who has what I call "social disease." We must remind ourselves that seventy percent of language is nonverbal. If we do not process nonverbal clues, we are missing a tremendous amount of information. We also need to understand how through nonverbal clues we cue expectations.

Now that you are equipped with tools and skills and experience, what next? What is your special outlook?

To pay more attention to general child development issues and concerns.

What is the next stage and what are the implications of when it gets muddled by a disability?

To focus on our expectations of going to college. We have started thinking about that. To continue to read. As we start having difficulties, we start trying again to understand what supports to kick in.

When the children were in elementary school, there seemed to be more commonality between my child and other children. As he gets older, he seems to feel more unique. It becomes more difficult to find understanding in a support group. This may be due to our change of focus—from looking at the problems to focusing on his strengths.

Every child's strengths will differ. In identifying ways of getting information when I need it, I have learned ways of advocating. I don't bring as much anxiety to the meetings. I've accepted.

I grew up in a very nurturing and supportive family. I thought that doing well was what life was like. That was my model of what it would be like to be a parent. There was no history in my family of disabilities, nothing to prepare me to be a parent of a child with a disability. I feel that through this experience, I am a better parent and teacher. I am grateful in a kind of way. My child has made me grow, he has been better for me as a professional. He has forced me to stretch in many ways that my other child has not challenged me. Some families have children who go through school without any major difficulties. Academically and socially their children do well. It is parents like that who do not understand what the challenges are for us and our children. They have no idea of the pain of isolation that parents feel, particularly in regards to social skills and social experiences. It is very painful when your child is never invited to birthday parties. When he was younger, I could arrange parties for my child, but the invitations were never reciprocated. By middle school, you can no longer orchestrate. You are dealing with a process and you try to understand how to help. These children are often very lonely.

As we move forward, how do you anticipate so that you can prepare yourself, and how do you prevent yourself from getting involved in worthless worrying?

What every parent wants for his or her child is for the child to be happy. Sometimes it can be scary to think that our children might never go away, will never become independent.

What strategies have you used to survive?

Educating myself in every way that I can. This includes reading, which I have already talked about. Also, I attend conferences and I take workshops that focus on how parents can support children with learning disabilities. There are lots of excellent presenters who focus on educating and supporting parents, such as Richard Lavoie, Mel Levine, Robert Brooks, and Ned Hallowell. I am also active in my local school system's council for parents of special needs children. I also make it my business to learn what my rights are as a parent and my child's rights under the law. I also make sure that I learn about the results of tests administered to my child. I found this very hard, especially at first, because the numbers and percentages didn't mean anything to me. I felt very uncomfortable about not understanding either what the tests meant or what their implications were for his learning. But, I also found that school and personnel and other people who assessed my son were very patient and very willing to help me understand. They didn't seem to mind when I asked the same questions over and over again, and I finally became more comfortable in my role as a parent asking questions until I understood.

My son has a hard time grasping abstract concepts, especially when he reads novels. He is a very concrete thinker. In terms of school, this has translated to mean that during the summer, he needs to read the books that he'll be reading in his English courses the coming year. By reading them for the first time during the summer, he can focus on the basic plot or story line; then, when he reads them again in class, he can focus on things like theme and character development, because he isn't confronting the "story" for the first time.

Another example is that his tests indicate that he has poor fine motor skills. His handwriting is horrendous, and when he focuses on good penmanship, the quality of his ideas in writing falls off because he can't pay attention to his penmanship and the ideas and organization all at the same time. It is my understanding that a person is not capable of performing two cognitive functions at the same time. For him, handwriting is a cognitive task because he has to consciously think about it to do it well, so when he's thinking about legible letter formation, he can't also think about what he wants to say. Once the person who assessed him explained this so that we could understand it, we were then able to advocate for him to learn keyboarding skills so that he could do all his writing on the word processor and thereby eliminate the need to struggle with handwriting most of the time.

Another thought about learning test results. We have found it very helpful to take notes when teachers and test people are talking to us about our son. Sometimes we think we are understanding things in the moment, but then we get home and we discover we still have questions. Having our notes is helpful because we can then talk more easily with the teachers or tester when we call them back for more explanations. No one has ever minded our taking notes or asking lots of questions because they don't expect us to be experts about test administration or interpretation.

I have also learned how important it is to know about how the school delivers services to students—whether the child will receive support in the class or be pulled out for individual instruction or small group instruction, or whether the special needs person will just consult with the class-room teacher to recommend modifications on materials or instruction. My husband and I found it helpful to understand the different services because we need to be able to weigh the pros and cons of each option in terms of our son's individual needs.

What has helped along the way?

Keeping careful track of information about our son, since, as his parents, we are the ones who are consistent, long-term monitors of his progress. We keep all the obvious things like educational plans and report cards and notes on conferences with teachers, tutors, and coaches. We also keep a journal of notes about what he likes to do and what he is having trouble with at different times.

I think it is also important to review my child's school cumulative folder every year before school ends in June. I as a parent have the right to see anything that is in my child's folder, and I have the right to remove certain types of information, such as negative, subjective comments, if I feel that they will negatively influence someone, such as next year's teacher, reading my child's folder. In my son's school, the school has always required that someone who is school personnel be with me when I do the review; that's fine with me because then they can answer questions that come up as I am looking through the folder.

What are your closing thoughts as to what you have learned from all of this?

In addition to all the other things I have mentioned, I have learned that I have to be an advocate for my child in areas other than just school. His disability doesn't just show up in the classroom. It shows up in sports, so I have to speak with the coaches. It shows up at camp, so I have to speak with the counselors. Sometimes I get worn out and aggravated by the job of advocating and wonder, "Does this ever end?" But I have found that in the long run both his life and mine go much more smoothly and he has fewer negative experiences if I communicate ahead of time with adults who work with him. That way, they have a context for thinking about his different ways of processing information and communicating, and they don't get so frustrated and upset. In turn, I don't feel miserable because yet another person has failed to understand his differences for what they are.

I used to think, long, long ago, that maybe I shouldn't tell teachers that my son has learning disabilities, because I was afraid that they would lower their expectations for him. But I quickly found out that if I didn't tell them, and if he was struggling, he became overwhelmed both by the tasks and by plummeting self-esteem. They didn't necessarily understand why he wasn't doing well. Some thought he was resistant; some thought he was dumb (the teacher's actual words were, "Maybe he's hit his learning ceiling"). Worst of all, our son assumed he was dumb and incapable. I have learned that what I need to do is tell the teachers about his disabilities and about what strategies are effective in helping him to compensate so that they don't have to lower standards for his performance but they do know how to support him appropriately so that he can be successful and achieve the standards they have set.

I have also learned to involve my son in all the conversations and information about his learning, because, ultimately, he is the one who is going to have to be responsible for his own learning and his own advocacy. He has learned to go up to his teachers at the end of class to make appointments when he doesn't understand something. He has learned to ask teachers to help him develop an outline for a paper before it's due, because he has trouble organizing his ideas. He has learned to keep all his assignments in a notebook and let us know in advance when he is going to need some help to complete an assignment.

And as part of involving him in knowing about himself, we have also helped him to pay attention to what he is good at, for two reasons. First of all, by knowing what he can do well, he can build on those strengths and try to find ways to use them when learning or improving a skill that is hard. Secondly, and maybe even more importantly, he needs to know what he does well—what Dr. Robert Brooks calls his "islands of competence"—so that he doesn't feel that he is just swimming in an "ocean of incompetence."

I have learned to go to meetings well prepared. I write down notes ahead of time on whatever I want to tell the teacher and any questions that I have. It's been helpful to do this, because I find that meetings can be a very emotional experience for me. If I don't plan ahead and make notes, then I can leave the meeting and discover that I didn't address what I had wanted to, either because I got sidetracked or because I got upset and forgot my original agenda.

We just interviewed a mother who didn't have a clue what to do at the team meeting, didn't know where to put the evaluation she was told to keep a copy of, and didn't know who to talk to. You, on the other hand, sound like you have it all together.

I have been at this for a lot longer. The only way I have come so far is by experience, reading, attending lectures, etc. I might sound like I know it all, but I will still buy every book out there that has to do with special needs, and not just my child's. There is always something to learn, some new way, or a different way of saying the same thing. That mother needs to do the same. She'll be "okay" as we all are.

Interview with Joni and Jane, Mothers of
Special Needs Children in Residential Settings

What has been the impact on the family of having a special needs child and what strategies have helped you to survive?

Joni: For our family, taking the step of considering and accessing residential treatment for our child has made a big difference. Maybe I should have considered it sooner. Our child was the youngest, and he was very disruptive and needy. It was a difficult step, but it has had an equalizing effect on the family.

It was a decision that I had to reach by myself. It was my decision with my husband's support. I believe he was ready for this step before I was.

Residential placement had been recommended when he was four years old, but at the time, I was not ready for that step. Now, with 20/20 vision, I feel I should have taken this step earlier. Now that I see a program that meets his needs, I see the value. He is happy.

Jane: With a child that has severe retardation and behavior problems, it might not take as long to make a decision to put your child in residential treatment. It is difficult to imagine the impact of the child's disability and difficulties on the rest of the kids in the family.

In terms of the siblings of a child with severe special needs, the best a family can look for is other adults to be around the kids and to openly acknowledge that the situation is bad. I can still see the impact and can openly acknowledge that the situation is bad. I can still see the impact that this experience has had on my other kids.

We gave her everything we knew we could give her, we accessed necessary services and programs. When the twins started to regress and we saw that the entire family was impacted, we had no choice.

Joni: Sometimes you reach this decision after you have exhausted all the other options.

Jane: Sometimes kids reach a time and a stage when it becomes necessary and appropriate to take this step. It should not be a decision that is reached under the gun.

Now that you are equipped with the tools to access the system and advocate for your child, what next? What is your outlook? What strategies do you need to keep going on?

Joni: This will vary from family to family. But what has worked for me and for my family is respite. To go away just with my husband. It is important to save the relationship.

Our goal for our son is that with enough training, we can gear him up for independent living. The school he is at now is helping with this process, but I need to prepare myself for this transition. I need to get information and understand what I need to know, so that I can prepare for this step.

Jane: I agree with Joni that it will vary from family to family. For me, the key words are activism and vigilance. You always need to keep your eyes open. Just because you are told that things are going well does not mean that you stop checking and asking questions.

You always want to be a savvy consumer. Evaluate programs and ask questions. A way to cope with the anger, frustration, and fear is to immerse yourself, find every bit of information available, investigate every lead. Channel this through advocacy. It is very rewarding to see things come to fruition.

The key is to be savvy, doubting, questioning, challenging, vigilant. If you need to be vigilant about normal children, you have to be even more so with special needs children.

We as parents have to be careful, also. We are so needy to hear good things, we can be vulnerable.

You have both become more and more involved with advocacy. How do you reassure other parents when they first contact you?

Jane: It is important to listen and to be sensitive. This is something Joni is very good at.

Ask questions and indicate by the questions you ask that you know and understand what you are talking about and that you have a sense of what these parents are going through.

You need to be educated about the population you are dealing with. That is why we have limited ourselves to working with parents of children with similar problems to our children. We can speak from experience.

In general?

Jane: Parents need to know the jargon before going out to negotiate for their child. You can use the jargon to question, challenge, and be treated as an equal. Reading available literature on a specific issue is one way to start familiarizing yourself with the jargon.

Parents should be careful—don't jump on the bandwagon when you hear there is a new treatment or program. We are a susceptible population. We need to ask questions and find out as much information as possible.

If you don't feel that a program or evaluation feels right, go with your instinct, your gut reaction. Beware of reports that call a child lazy or manipulative.

Interview with Judy, Mother of Four Children, Each with a Special Need

You have more than one child with special needs in the family. What impact has this had on your family? What strategies have helped you to survive?

I have had to be more organized to keep up with everyone's records. I need to be able to access information about the children when teachers, doctors, and counselors ask specific questions. It does not all fit into a baby book anymore.

It has impacted our daily schedule and routine. The schedule has had to revolve around their special needs. For example, homework. With one child, it might mean reading the assignment to him, transcribing notes, or helping to organize notes. With another, it might mean helping with research—he just can't go to the library and get it. Another might need some direction. It is more than providing a special place to do their homework and structured time in the afternoon or evening for doing their assignments. It is about being directly involved in some of the tasks.

It has impacted my work, which is now them. I have not been able to work outside the home. They need constant supervision some of the time. Sometimes it means going to each school once a week. There have been times in the past where I have been in one school three or four times a week to address different issues or meet with different staff members.

Of the skills that you have had to develop, what has been more difficult and what has helped?

Each child has his own set of needs, and I have had to research and advocate for each child individually. With some, it was strictly medical issues; others were a combination of medical, social, and school-related issues; others were strictly school-related.

Learning to advocate has helped. Learning to advocate with other parents and support groups has also helped.

How have you assisted other parents?

By sharing information and experiences, by helping others access resources, by volunteering with a variety of organizations. Not all the organizations are special needs, but I network with people wherever I am about special needs.

Has networking with organizations that are not primarily for special needs made a difference?

Parents with children that have special needs go to lots of places. You tend to find people who have similar issues.

With changes in the law, organizations have had to become more sensitive to those issues and are always looking for parents that are more vocal and can help them adapt their program to meet the needs of their child.

What do you do to allay parents' fears and anxieties when you speak to them?

The biggest fear is that their child will be seen differently. By saying that I have been there and my child is not seen differently has helped. It is a good way to diminish fear.

Another fear is "How do I get the services my child needs?" You can help other parents feel less fearful by helping them advocate for their child, by showing them how to access services, and by making them feel empowered as a professional. I emphasize professional because that is what they are. They know their child better than anyone else. They need to know that they are the professionals. There are too many people out there who might try to sweep the parent under the rug.

What are common needs of parents?

All parents need to know their rights regarding the development and implementation of the IEP. Parents should look for help from other parents when getting an educational plan. It is not only the school that can provide input. The biggest need that goes unmet for the parent is respite—a time to recharge. I think single parents in particular don't get that.

Assess other resources that are available, whether a soccer program, scouts, or a special program.

What have you learned from this experience that has been valuable?

The biggest thing that I have learned is that having a child with special needs is not the end of the world. That was my feeling in the beginning. As my kids are growing, graduating, and going into the work force, they are not seen as "special needs"; their special needs are no longer the focus.

I have also learned to develop and tap on a strength that I never knew I had. I have learned to develop skills I never thought I could develop.

I see myself differently than before. I guess I see myself as more professional, more knowledgeable, and more willing to learn. I have matured!

What else would you like to tell parents?

See yourself as a professional, and don't be afraid to look for new resources. Don't be afraid to help adapt existing resources. Just because a program does not advertise that it will meet a special need does not mean that they cannot or are not willing to adapt their services.

Be willing to network with other people, to tap other parents. Some have been where you are going, and some are going where you have been.

Be organized and keep records. That has saved us so many times. Just to be able to pull out the documentation when you need to or to see for yourself the changes, the growth. Sometimes you are so caught up in the process that you do not notice the changes.

Listening to you reminds me of things we have written about in this book. It sounds at times as if you have already read our book.

No, I have not read it, I just have lived it.

Would a book like this have been of some help, and if so, why and how?

When my oldest child began having problems in school, I had no idea how to help him. The school offered some services, but they were not meeting his needs. I believed that these services were all they could offer. I looked for books that could help me, but there was very little on the market. A book like this might have helped me get the services he needed earlier. This kind of book is more that just informational, it gives support.

Interview with Ruth, Mother of a Child with Mild Special Needs, Who Is in the Process of a Divorce

Ruth, thank you for sharing your thoughts. What has it been like emotionally to deal with your special needs child?

I have found it the most frustrating, the most challenging, and mostly the most rewarding experience. I see life in a completely different way. I understand a broader spectrum of life.

How so?

I have a better sense of people with disabilities, and more than that I understand about taking things for granted. For example, you know those sinks whose faucets you have to hold while washing your hands? Well, my son only has one hand to work with, so if he is holding the faucet, how can he wash his hand? These things are frustrating, like fitting a square peg into a round hole. You can't change the world, but you can try, and you can make a difference in speaking out for the things you believe in and want to change, although you can't run around calling every building changing faucets. In a case like this, you need to try to make it universal, get a bill introduced, adding it to handicapped facilities, things like that. I get really upset. I want the world to fit for my child, and it doesn't.

How has all this affected your home life?

Well, you know what's going on. The thing that upsets me the most is that so many people assume that the marriage failed because of our child. That infuriates me as much as the faucets. Our marriage was never a strong one, and having a special needs child was just one of many stresses that tore us apart. It's not like we had a great marriage and along comes this special needs child and boom, we split like an atom. If anything, while the child was going through some of his more critical times, we were actually drawn together. I've been told by people that oftentimes a special needs situation can either bring you a lot closer or tear you apart. In my case, it didn't really do either; it all averaged out. I don't know what makes people divorce in all cases, but the problems that drove us apart came long before the child was even diagnosed.

How do you feel about being on your own with a special needs child? Or I shouldn't say on your own, but really as a single parent.

Well, I won't be the first mother or father in this situation, and definitely not the last. I guess as with anything, the family dynamics will change, but the stresses will too. In some ways, there will probably be more stress, since I will have custody, so I will be doing the more ongoing daily tasks; but on the other hand, the stresses that were in the house before will be gone. Here, too, it will average out. I don't really feel I'll be losing a support system, since I usually found my support more through other parents, teachers, and counselors.

Like my special needs child, who was diagnosed at age three, I have learned that life didn't deal me the cards I thought I would get, and I've learned how to adjust and face the many challenges. I'll just have to do this with my personal life, as well.

Interview with Karyn, Mother of a Child with
both Medical and Learning Special Needs

Can you give me some basic feelings of what you have been going through? I know your child has both medical and learning problems.

Basically, it's been a challenging yet successful journey. We have tried, although it's been difficult at times, to balance it all. I know that sounds like a general statement, and it is, but in the end that really is what you do—try to put it all together, mix it up, and come out with the right balance. My heart breaks for my child. Life is hard for her and I wish I could magically make it better. But I can't make the world right for her, nor for my other children who have no special needs. I can only give my children the best, the foundations, the values, and hope that the world treats them and receives them in a way I want it to. It's especially hard for her because I think she is so much more vulnerable. Special needs parents don't come with magic snapping fingers to make the problems disappear, we only come with love and knowledge, which we get with books like yours!

Thanks for the compliment. That is our intention with this book, to help parents like you. What about your family life—how has a special needs child affected that?

Sometimes you'd never know there was a special needs child in the family, and other times, well . . . it's unbelievable.

How so?

For one thing, my husband and I do not agree on how to approach many of her special needs issues. Parents don't come with automatic contracts that they are going to agree on everything with child rearing. We don't agree on issues with our other two, and this spills over with the special needs child.

Do you mind sharing some of that?

Not at all, that's why I agreed to the interview. I don't know about other parents, but I need to talk and share my feelings and see that others are going through the same things that I am. It really does help take the isolation out of it, and more importantly, it helps me realize that I'm okay, that what I'm feeling or doing isn't something from outer space! (At least I still have my sense of humor.) Anyway, our basic disagreement is how we view her special needs. Our child falls between the cracks; she's in the mild range, not very handicapped yet not really in the "normal" world. My husband tends to push her into the more handicapped world, and I tend to push her more towards the normal world, trying to make that normal world fit her special needs world. Sometimes we come to real blows with this. I believe in reaching for the highest denominator, reaching up. My husband wants to put her in the other world. It's frustrating. I'm sure there are many children who fall in this area, and it's hard being neither here nor there. I wish I could create a third world of mild special needs for her. I guess it doesn't really work that way.

How do the other children take it?

For the most part, they deal with it very well. We have basic rules, such as if the children get mad at each other, nothing related to the special needs can be addressed. Not that I'm advocating teasing, I just mean that if they're having a discussion or fight, they can't what I call "attack" with the sensitive areas. I'm getting long-winded, but basically my daughter has some facial paralysis, very very slight, but her smile is a little crooked. So, no one can ever say anything about that in anger. I also tend to not give my other children any specific tasks around the house—it's just my own personal philosophy. I feel that when I need help with my special needs child, I ask the others to pitch in, maybe it's helping put on her brace, or something, but they are always willing to help, and I feel that is their responsibility, and it's hard enough to have a special needs child in the family, they don't need other responsibilities. I know there are parents that would disagree with me, but that's my philosophy.

That's okay. It's okay to have different philosophies. What do you see for her future?

I see a long and happy one, but one with challenges. The thing that gets me a lot is areas I forget about and don't think about every day. Then there are the things that won't be happening for a long time—I find myself worrying about them now.

Can you give me an example of each?

I was cutting her fingernails (she can't cut her left hand because her right hand is weakened). She asked me who was going to cut her nails when she grew up. The question really took me by surprise. I had given lots of thought to what she will do when she graduates high school, but this was a specific question that gave me a jolt. Then, there are the things I worry about way down the road, like if she'll be able to be on her own at college, or what she'll do for a job. I guess the best way I can sum it up is to say I think you need to take one day at a time and take one future at time, if that makes any sense.

Conclusion

As we all know, sharing personal information with the outside world can be rather difficult. Though we may be used to talking to others about some of our issues, it is a big jump to open up and allow a broader audience to share our innermost private thoughts and experiences.

These interviews are a window through which others can get a glimpse or a closer look at special parents. Most are still struggling, though at different levels and intensities, with the ongoing process of raising their child and of dealing with the complexities brought about by their child's special needs. But, as these parents face their own issues and reality, they also wish to pave the road in any way possible for other parents or to expedite the accessing of information or services that can be beneficial to their children.

Parents experience the process of accessing services in many different ways. Some of these differences will be due to the nature and severity of a child's special needs. Other differences will reflect variation in service delivery across states or among school districts. Some parents will travel through this process with many positive experiences, while others will feel that they are in a continuous battle. But every parent will be a changed person because of these experiences.

These interviews help to personalize the world of special needs. Too often, people forget that behind the demographics, percentages, labels, and evaluations are human faces—a real family and real children. Parental participation plays a crucial role in the process of special education. Without the opportunity to voice our experiences, the participation and the process would seem remote and sometimes cold. Parents of children with special needs need to hear from one another, and other parents in our communities and specialists in the field need to understand our reality.

We hope these interviews give you an overview of some of the emotions that special needs parents are dealing with, how they are coping, the common threads that you share, and the universal emotions with which you can identify.

10

Things We Never Even Thought About

We're given the news. Whether it's from a doctor, a teacher, a counselor, or another source, we receive information that isn't part of our dreams for the future. Nevertheless, we have to deal with what we are told, even if we want to deny it, and we deal with it every step of the way, in every way.

This chapter will look at areas of life and everyday living that we may take for granted. Throughout this book, we have focused on the medical, educational, recreational, and emotional aspects of the child with special needs, and we have explored ways to access services as well as support the child in these different worlds. As we struggle with these special needs of our child, we often fail to realize the ramifications of his disability in other areas of his life. Special needs isn't always compartmentalized; it permeates into every area of our lives, from the school to the home. It doesn't end when they graduate, it doesn't end when they become legal adults; it doesn't end. As we walk down the roads in this journey, we start facing things we never thought about.

These children live in a world far beyond our wildest imagination, and the better prepared we are, the better prepared they will be. In the next few pages, we highlight some topics that we have identified through personal accounts, interviews, and research. This is in no way an all-inclusive list, but it may achieve these important goals:

- You will have an awareness of other aspects of your child's life that will eventually need your attention.
- You will start thinking about other concerns brought about by your child's disability.
- You will start to slowly prepare yourself by asking questions and locating resources.

In talking with other parents, we have come to realize that there are many issues that may not often be considered. This chapter does not present an extensive exploration of the issues, just a brief introduction that also illustrates how a child's disability permeates other areas of his life.

Driving

The unexpected comes in just that way—it's startling. A future worry can be brought up at any time, anywhere. Something will trigger it. For instance, in the case of driving, the following scenario occurred.

Sandy: My daughter Rayna was only seven, and I was just dealing with the idea of school, IEP, other special services, etc. We were on our way to camp, and out of the clear blue, as we were stopped at a red light, Rayna suddenly asked, "Mommy, am I ever going to be able to drive?" It's a good thing that I was stopped at a red light, because I was so taken aback by this question.

If it is at all possible for the child to be able to drive, there are schools with handicapped automobiles. You just need to call these schools and inquire about them.

Traveling with a Special Needs Child

Traveling with children is one experience of life; traveling with special needs children is a different experience altogether. Traveling in general comes with its own set of variables; if you add special needs to this, then like everything else in dealing with a special needs child, this too is dealt with and experienced in a different way.

Sandy: Most places are handicap-accessible and/or very oriented to the handicapped, but there is also the case of my special needs child. Rayna is not wheelchair-bound, yet she wears a leg brace and has difficulty walking long distances. I have taken some steps when traveling to facilitate her mild, yet essential, needs and to make traveling easier for her.

I call ahead to where we are staying. If it is a hotel, I ask for a room as close to the elevator as possible. In some hotels, you must travel long winding corridors from the elevator to reach the room. If it is a motel, I also see if a first floor is available, which would eliminate the steps. If we are staying at a resort, I ask for a room as close to the pool or dining room or whatever facility will be used the most. (If you are staying at a large resort where you will be spending equal amounts of time at the different facilities, you have to decide which facility is the most advantageous to be close to.) I always opt for the swimming pool, in case Rayna wants to go back and forth from the room.

When flying, I usually ask for a seat up front, to avoid walking down the long passageways in planes. Sometimes you might want to be seated all the way to the back, because in some planes this is where the bathrooms are located, and one long trip back and forth upon boarding and deplaning is better than back and forth several times to use the bathrooms. The best thing to do is ask your travel agent or the airline about the layout of the airplane before asking for seating assignment. You can make your own decisions, based on your needs. I also ask for an aisle seat. Rayna's right leg tends to go out, and she finds it easier to have more space; or I ask for the very first seat, which gives the most leg room. (I also always request aisle seats when attending the theater or wherever seats can be assigned ahead of time.)

Don't be afraid to make your needs known. On a recent train trip to New York City, while traveling alone with Rayna, I knew I wouldn't be able to negotiate her on the steps as well as the luggage. The porters are always there to help you up and down the steps, but I needed someone to help carry the luggage through the train station so I could help her on any stairs, etc. I told the conductor my situation and that I needed help. He called ahead and had a porter waiting for me with a cart to put the luggage on. My hands were free, and I could help Rayna.

We recognize the frustrations that can occur while traveling. But just maintain the same attitude that you have with everything else in life, that because you have someone in the family with special needs, you must approach things from a different vantage point. And that's all it is, a different vantage point—there is no reason why traveling can't be fun and enjoyable. It just involves a different set of blueprints when planning it out. And we truly believe that the key to a successful vacation is planning it out in advance. Just as in the IEP meetings, the doctor's appointments, networking, advocacy, and every other aspect of your child's life, the more prepared you are, the better your experience. Knowing the right questions to ask doesn't always come easily; but once you set a pattern, keep it.

Sandy: On a recent vacation, we selected a resort. I made sure to tell the person taking reservations that I needed a room near the pool. I told her I had a daughter with a disability who had trouble walking, so I wanted to be near the pool in case she wanted to go back and forth to the room. When we arrived, we found they had indeed put us near a pool, but their definition of close and my definition did not match. I realized I wasn't specific enough, that the room was around the opposite side of the building with a small incline. This small incline and extra distance would have made it difficult for Rayna, who agewise was old enough to go back and forth to the room, but disability-wise was not. We had to rearrange the rooms and were lucky that something else was available.

Our best advice is to keep this information with all your travel information. Among the maps, airline information, and guidebooks, keep a sheet with the "right" questions to ask. You may stumble a little at first, but the more seasoned traveler you become, the better you'll be with questions and requests. Rely on your travel agent; make your needs specific. Here, too, ask friends: network with them, reach out for the same support you have received in other areas. Ask about good places to travel, what they know about the accommodations, and what experiences they may have had that can add to the pleasure of your trip, and avoid some of the negative experiences. Traveling can be a wonderful experience for everyone.

Sexuality

Depending on the special needs of your child, this area might be handled similarly to the way many people prepare their children on this subject, or it might require a lot of thought and preparation. Some children with special needs can be overtrusting or have a limited capacity to grasp the concept of sexuality. They can be at risk of being abused by others, of being sexually exploited. Thus, as parents you may need to arm yourselves with much information and support, as dictated by your child's special needs. As the child turns into an adult, the issues of marriage and children may need to be considered.

Some parents may have to search for books that present information in a manner that facilitates the child's understanding of the information, in other words, books that are written at the child's level of comprehension. Several organizations provide parents with specific resources.

When the Doctor Moves, Retires, or Dies

When an illness or a problem puts us in the hands of another to help us deal with that problem, we find that we are dependent and vulnerable. We depend on a certain doctor; we rely on his judgment, expertise, and his help, in whatever way it can be imparted. Sometimes we may forget that this person is still just a human being. This person can move, retire, or even die, which can have a devastating impact on the special needs child, the parents, perhaps the whole family. You can take several steps to help prepare against such a problem, not to erase the inevitability but to help smooth the road if something happens.

Sandy: We spent many hours researching a doctor when Rayna was first diagnosed. We ran with reports, X rays, and hope, seeking out one doctor after another, looking for everything in one doctor: someone we felt comfortable with, who could give us the compassion we were so desperately longing for, and deep down inside we hoped for someone who could tell us it was all a bad dream, and nothing was wrong with Rayna. No one told us it was a bad dream, but after a great deal of searching, we finally decided on a doctor we felt comfortable with. Having done thorough research, we decided on a neurologist who could help us, and we felt better at once and were satisfied that we had made the right decision.

After four years of steady appointments and steady satisfaction, the unexpected happened. Rayna's wonderful doctor announced that in six months he would be leaving to take a position as head of pediatric neurology at another hospital. We were totally devastated and felt extremely vulnerable. We had several options: choosing among other doctors recommended at that hospital, finding a completely new doctor on our own, or continuing with this doctor in his new setting. We opted for the last, but because it really wasn't feasible to have our main doctor so far away, we also asked him for recommendations. Now we alternate between the two doctors, the local one and the original one.

Once a year we travel to the original doctor's facility for Rayna's checkup. We even make a minivacation out of the trip, using the opportunity to see different parts of the country. We recognize that this option isn't always possible, but it is something to consider.

Moving away with a Special Needs Child

Moving in itself has many traumatic facets and involves adjustments for any child. When you are dealing with a special needs child, the move can become even more monumental. With some moves, you have the choice of what town or state you go to and you can be selective about the school. This can involve much research, networking, and utilization of the tools we have discussed in this book. In other cases, because of one reason or another, such as a job transfer, you may not have the luxury of being so selective when looking for the appropriate school for the child.

The best way to talk about this subject is to share a conversation we had with Alice, whose husband was transferred out of state, about two thousand miles away. She was to move from a heavily populated area with many options for her son's special needs to a smaller setting where the choices were limited. While federal regulations require that every public school system offer a free and appropriate education to the special needs child, the situation can be difficult in some geographical areas.

It is surprising to learn what can happen when a family has to face the issue of moving away, whether to the next town, the next state, or several thousand miles away. This is one of those things that you never think about until the situation crops up, and it can be very overwhelming in the best of circumstances.

Alice, what was your first reaction when you found out that David might be transferred?

Total panic. That's the only word I can think of. How would I ever find a school for Jeff? I had just settled him in the special needs school; I had mediated with the town, and they were in complete agreement that he would be better off in that environment. Jeff had been there for only one year before I found out that David needed to move. David's company was willing to help in any way, but I was still panicked. Talk about transitions. Jeff had just transitioned to this new school, and luckily he was still doing well, but I was supposed to uproot him and take him not only out of this school, but away from his friends as well. I wasn't very happy. The other problem was that I couldn't let his current school know what was going on, because spaces in this school are such a premium, with so many people wanting to fill limited spaces, that I was afraid to let them know we might be leaving. So I couldn't rely on them for information or support.

What did you do? Tell me step by step.

First, I went to the library here and researched all the private schools in the new area. I looked at special needs schools and nonspecial needs schools. I read everything there was to read about schools in that state. A lot of schools were eliminated right away, some because of the religious affiliation and others because they were not appropriate for Jeff in various ways, such as being high-powered. I was then left with a small number of schools that were hopefuls. I cross-referenced these schools to find out which ones had special needs services.

I then called the State Department of Education and explained my situation to them. I gave them my son's history and asked for recommendations. They had me call the special education director in the town that we were looking to live in. I called her, and she talked to me about the various programs. She suggested one private school that she thought would be good to consider.

I called this private school and spoke to them. It turned out it was much too small and confining. The entire school from first through twelfth grade only had fifty students. I knew my son wouldn't thrive in this kind of environment. The school gave me the name of another school, so I called them, and it turned out that my son was too advanced. His disability wasn't severe enough. I had panicked before, but now I really started to panic.

My husband went to the new town on weekends to start looking for housing and to meet with his client. He came home with the Yellow Pages. I looked up some religious institutions and called a spiritual leader there who was most helpful and supportive. But unfortunately, he recommended those same two schools.

I was left with only two alternatives for schools, neither of which was satisfactory. One was a school at the other end of the state, where Jeff would have to board. That option was unacceptable. The other school was actually in the next state, two hours away from David's job, therefore we could live in the middle and each would have a one-hour commute. I thought that was much too long to add to Jeff's school day.

It sounds like a no-win situation. What did you do?

We decided that I would live here with the two kids and keep Jeff in his special needs school, and David would commute (a three-hour plane ride). We had been working very closely with David's company and told them up front what was going on and why we needed to make this split. We chronicled all the steps we had taken in endeavoring to seek education for Jeff, and we told them of our decision to stay up here. We gave a list of proposals to David's company. We asked for compensation for David to commute home every weekend and for us to go down on vacations and in the summer, and to pay for David's apartment and a live-in person to help me take care of the kids in David's absence. The company agreed to all of this. David and I felt this was the best decision. I went down with him one weekend to help him look for a small apartment. At that time, the client informed David's company that he had completely changed his mind and wasn't going to pursue the project, and David never had to move!

What a story. Do you live in fear now that this could possibly happen again?

All the time. In fact, the company is not doing well now. The situation I described to you took place three years ago. I live in fear that we will have to move to chase after a job, and we'll have to go through this nightmare all over again.

Alice's interview brings up so many issues. In their case, they were very lucky to be working with such a successful company at the time, and David's position was so much in demand that the company was willing to give them such compensations. But this is not always the case. Many people have to leave a town and seek employment in other places, and they run into the same situation as Alice in finding the right school. Of course, the outcome might work in your favor, so that you move away and find a facility even more appropriate and more rewarding than you ever anticipated. It does not always have to be a negative experience, but the accompanying anxiety and frustration can be very difficult.

Not all moves will be the same, and not all situations will be as difficult as it was for Alice and her family. The best advice we can offer is to hone your networking skills. Call upon those resources, put them to use not forgetting the advocating techniques. You may not have total control over where you go, where you send your child to school, or what programs will be available, but you can still advocate and speak up for what your child needs.

Money Management

As you strive to make your child more independent, one of the skills you try to develop is his understanding of money as well as his ability to manage it effectively. Children with special needs will vary greatly in their capacity to master this skill, from never being capable to being totally capable. As our children grow and develop, we need to take a look at what impact their disability has on this issue. Some situations will require that you teach them money management skills (for example, allow a certain amount of money in a bank account, or issue a credit card with a small limit), how to use a checkbook, and ways of budgeting their money and keeping track of their expenses. Other situations may require you to consider such issues as a trust or a legal guardianship.

Related to money management is the issue of accepting solicitations, if your child does not have a legal guardian. Advertisements and telephone solicitation calls can wreak havoc if the special needs child says yes to these calls and obligates you for money. Making sure that the special needs child doesn't sign anything that will obligate you for money commitments is also an issue.

Illness in the Family

We struggle to cope with the reality and demands brought about by our child's special needs; life, meanwhile, does not let us keep other difficulties and stressors out. Sometimes our hectic schedule, limited flexibility, and energy is taxed by other illnesses in the family. Some illnesses might be short-term and not life-threatening; others may be long-term and of a serious nature, or terminal. It may be another child in the family, your parents, in-laws, or any other member of the extended family. Whatever the case, it will demand your attention, energy, and time.

This scenario may occur more often than we care to think about, but like any other bad news we must face, we eventually have to deal with it. This is a time when you must put in place some support systems if you have not already, or you might need to activate those you use on an as-needed basis, or you might temporarily need to increase them. You need to look clearly at what impact this situation is having on a family already taxed by the special needs of the child or children. Clearly understanding the impact of the illness on the family will allow you to start identifying the kind of support that you and your family might need to survive this situation.

You, the parent, may need support in the form of respite care, to allow time to refuel; it might be in the form of counseling, to give you an opportunity to vent your feelings and explore ways to cope with a very difficult situation; it might be in the form of a support group where you find others who share and understand your situation and with whom you can explore alternatives or resources; it might be a combination of all of the above. For certain families, it might require that the children access some support system as well; and in some cases, the family might benefit from family sessions.

If the illness presently has no impact on the family but will become more serious and difficult down the road, do not wait until later to start accessing or activating support. The sooner you prepare yourself for what is ahead, the better able you will be to recognize signals in the family indicating a need for some type of support or intervention. Do not wait for a crisis to take action. Be as proactive as you can.

Stress can be very detrimental, affecting our health, coping mechanism, personal relationships, and so on—depleting us emotionally and physically. Recognize early that there are limitations to what we can do and that it is important and necessary to seek and accept help.

Information and skills we have presented throughout this book will become even more necessary during difficult times. You must be organized and know where you have important information or documents; you must access support systems and use any technology that is affordable and assists you to simplify your life to keep daily routines intact.

Parents Aging or Dying

When we discover that our child has special needs, we start to prepare ourselves for the here and now. Our focus and energy is directed toward accessing immediate services, support, information, and resources.

At some point, every parent contemplates the thought and experiences the fear of the dreaded questions: "What if something happens, and I will not be around to raise my children, to see them grow? Who will be there to guide them and protect them if I am not around?"

For some of us, it might be a passing thought that is quickly pushed aside. For other parents, due to health issues that they face or because they have a special needs child requiring lifelong care, these questions become very relevant and not just a passing thought.

If the child's special needs are in the more severe range of disability, then the concern over his care and welfare becomes more pressing as the parents get older. Modern medicine has extended the life span of many children with special needs, and thus we need to be concerned about their adult care. As parents age, they may eventually become less capable of taking care of their offspring. Thought and plans for the child's care need to be given to this possibility, ideally long before it becomes a reality.

Though none of us like to think about death or a stage in our life where we can no longer be self-sufficient, we cannot postpone facing this fact. We may need to look at facilities that care for older individuals with special needs and find out their requirements and costs. What is available in the state? Do you need to place your child on a waiting list, or do you need to start taking steps by the time your child reaches a certain age? Should you look at respite care, state residential schools or institutions, residential/ community homes, or private residential programs?

Dwindling funds and limited resources have made many of the above options scarce in many states and communities. By the time parents feel ready to look at these options, they may find that nothing is available for them and for their child. Thus, parents should start considering this stage of life long before they are even close to this cycle. Though it may seem logical that a society that recognizes the needs and rights of individuals with disabilities and provides for free and appropriate public education would consider and provide services to cover the full life span of these individuals, that is not necessarily a given in our present society.

Socialization

We know that children need to interact with peers and others in order to develop social skills necessary to integrate and function successfully in our society. Having children join play groups, invite friends over, and go to a friend's house are activities that every parent and child is involved in or expects to be involved in as part of the natural process of growing up and learning to socialize with others.

For many parents of children with special needs, this seemingly easy and common task may be much more difficult than they ever dreamed possible. They may find that some parents do not feel comfortable around children with certain disabilities, thus they do not reach out to include the parent and/or the special needs child in normal outings; or some of these other parents may not reciprocate your invitations or overtures at establishing friendships and connections for your child.

Sometimes parents may find it difficult to find a play group that is appropriate or inclusive of children with special needs, or they might locate play groups too far away, thus curtailing the usefulness of such a program.

Sometimes teachers may not realize that some children with special needs have difficulties with social skills because they may not pick up social cues or nonverbal messages from their peers and surrounding environment. Consequently, these children might have difficulty establishing friendships or sustaining relationships unless there is some direct and active assistance on the teacher's part in helping the special needs child make connections with other children and negotiate relationships. For some of these children, just being in a classroom with other children or in a playground is not enough, and leaving it up to the children to work it out on their own will not work.

Not all children with special needs will have a problem with socialization and forming and sustaining friendships. But for some children, this might be another area in which they will struggle, causing frustration and pain for both the parents and the child. Parents may need to find creative and resourceful ways to provide their child with opportunities to be with other children. It may require finding organizations within the school or community in which your child can participate or accessing services such as Big Brother or Big Sister.

After-School Care

Again, finding the necessary programs or services may be very difficult. After-school programs for children with special needs may be few or nonexistent in some communities. Programs might be available, but they might have a limited amount of available space, or they may not provide the necessary transportation or have the necessary accessibility.

As mentioned by one of the parents we interviewed, it sometimes might be necessary to negotiate with some organizations on an individual basis for an opening for your child. With some information and support on the part of the parents, some programs may be willing to extend their services to children with special needs.

Parental involvement and advocacy will play a central role in accessing and extending after-school services to children with special needs. For many working parents, this may be a necessary service, and for many children with special needs it is an opportunity to interact with other children in a nonacademic setting where other skills and experiences are developed.

Religious Rites of Passage

As with everything else in the life of your special needs child, religious rites of passage may be experienced just a little bit differently than usual. If it is something that you must prepare for, check with your religious institution to see if the ceremony can be modified in ways to meet the needs of the child.

Just remember that this is a special time in your child's life, and regardless of the way in which it is observed, the fact remains that it can be observed and celebrated. Your child is special and has had to do so many other things in life differently, just take the positives and cling to the successes.

Dietary Restrictions

Dietary restrictions, even in the best of circumstances, for any kind of person, can have a large impact on one's life. Lactose intolerance, wheat allergies, whatever the case may be, is just one more component in life to deal with. The only difference here is that if your special needs child has the dietary restriction, then having one more thing to deal with can be very difficult.

Health is at stake here. If the special needs child is at risk by eating a certain food and mistakenly eats it, the results can be serious. The best advice we can offer is to make a list of the products that your child can eat, and always make sure you have those products readily available, especially when away from home. Share this information with the parents of your child's friends and tell them what to do in case of an emergency and how to reach you. Provide them with a specific list of foods that your child cannot have.

Housing

Another long-term consideration that may have never crossed your mind is where your special needs child will live when he reaches an age that you feel or he feels he should be on his own. There are many facilities for sheltered living, umbrella situations, and here, too, you need to do your research. In this case, this research should be initiated at a fairly early stage, because there can be waiting list situations.

Start by calling your local government offices and ask about housing situations. Also, if you are considering guardianship, a lawyer can probably give you information.

Occupation

This is a broad area: what your child will do after school. Here, too, depending on the severity of the disability, different doors will be opened—and closed.

Many employment opportunities and facilities have special programs for the special needs person. The school that the child has been attending is the best place to start to talk about occupations. Remember, federal law stipulates that prior to a child turning sixteen, transition services must be provided and written in the child's IEP. Transition services include school to post-school activities, such as post-secondary education, vocational training, integrated employment, continuing and adult education, adult services, independent living, and community participation.

Humor

We conclude this chapter with a section on humor, because it is something that we never give enough attention to or at times tend to easily dismiss. Life is a challenge; that is something we somberly acknowledge. This does not preclude the ability to laugh, however. Some people may feel uncomfortable about this, perhaps because the notion of enjoying life in the face of such seriousness seems to be a contradiction. But laughter is good. It can help you face the everyday seriousness, and it can be a great comfort. Don't be afraid to laugh, don't be afraid to enjoy life, and most of all, don't be afraid to laugh when something funny occurs in relation to your child's special needs. This is the most important aspect of the chapter that we want to emphasize.

Sandy: I have one favorite humorous story in relation to Rayna's problems. I was taking Rayna to the hospital to have an MRI, at that time also referred to as an NMR. Bypassing the information desk, I walked through the corridors of the hospital, sure I knew where to go. Suddenly, I stopped short. I didn't have the foggiest idea how to find the room. Spotting two doctors walking down the corridor, I stopped them, and asked where I could find the NMR.

"You want an enema?" (No, but instead I'll take a healthy daughter.)

When I started to repeat NMR, I realized I was about to do something I hadn't done in almost two months: laugh. It did help, and it did make me feel better for at least a minute or two. I repeated my story to Rayna.

"He thought I said 'en-e-ma.' Get it?

See, honey, the initials N-M-R can sound like en-e-ma, and an enema is when . . ."

Something we always think about: that the Things We Never Even Thought About list is endless.

11

Special Highlights

Our hope in writing this book is for you to have a resource guide, a referral guide, an informational guide—a support system in the written word and a source of inspiration to carry with you throughout life. Our intention is that you read the book once through, then you can refer to it whenever you need a reminder, or a lift, or a gentle dose of inspiration and hope. But we acknowledge how busy your lives are, especially when coping with issues of disabilities, and we realize that reading the book again and again might not be feasible.

Therefore, we have decided to include a chapter highlighting the key elements of this book, which you can refer to when you're in a pinch and want a quick reminder. For instance, if you're off to a doctor's appointment and want to remember some of the key points in the chapter, "The Special Needs Child in the Medical World," you can scan a list rather than rereading the entire chapter. In a sense, we have "highlighted" the book for you. So, now that you've nearly completed the book, rest assured that you can just flip to this chapter and scan the key elements of each chapter, then focus in on exactly what you need at a certain time.

Chapter 2: Getting Organized

Organization is the key to eliminating some of the many frustrations that you are faced with.

It's important to keep all reports.

Get organized and stay organized.

Establish a secure record-keeping system.

Record Keeping

Keep a separate section for everything related to your child's special needs.

Keep all your information in one area.

Use subject dividers to separate the different categories.

Place papers chronologically and put the dates in bold letters on top of the various reports.

Identify the school year across the top.

Keeping Copies

Keep copies of all reports—never send anything out without copying it first (ask for two copies when receiving a report).

If you're copying at a public place, wait for it.

Have two-sided copies made, saving space and helping the environment.

Equipment and Supplies

Get as much office equipment at home as is feasible: telephone answering machine, copy machine, fax machine, typewriter, computer, beeper, car phone.

Use the answering machine as a message center within the home besides answering outside telephone calls.

Screen the answering machine calls when you want peace and quiet.

Call-waiting is a valuable tool, allowing you to receive calls and still use the telephone; or a second telephone line is helpful.

A beeper and a cellular telephone are also helpful.

Keep office supplies on hand: envelopes, mailers, labels, stamps.

Telephone Directory

Include the doctor's name, telephone number, specialty, secretary's name, and who referred you.

Loose-leaf style is more practical, making changes or deletions easier.

Bring the telephone directory to the team meeting so you can give information immediately.

Calendar

Bring the calendar with you to all appointments.

Write long-term dates across the top.

Note long-term return calls (for example, if you are told to call the doctor back in two weeks, put that down on the calendar).

Note who the appointment is for (more than one person in the family may see the same doctor).

When writing an appointment in the calendar for a core or a doctor's appointment, etc., make an entry two weeks earlier (or as much time as you need) so you can start preparing mentally and write down any thoughts or questions that come up.

Check the calendar every day to get yourself organized for the next day.

Organizing

It's okay to delegate tasks to others.

Try to build in down time or leisure time.

If you're better organized, you're in a better position to help your child.

Teach your child organization skills.

Chapter 3: Networking

Networking is the exchange of ideas and information.

You may not have networking skills now, but they can be successfully developed.

Climb out of your shell and meet people.

Find programs, schools, and camps.

Find support systems.

Networking Rules

Never throw out any information.

If your first attempt at a source fails, don't give up—there are no dead ends.

Follow every lead, no matter how inconsequential they may seem.

Always be active—you are the primary tool in networking.

Sources for Networking

Telephone book, white and yellow pages

Teachers, doctors, and therapists

Peers

Mailing lists, reference books, publications, and the media

Courses, lectures, and organizations

Telephone Strategies in Networking

Make telephone calls at a quiet time.

Always have pencil and paper handy.

Always write down the name of the person to whom you are speaking, as well as their extension.

When you call an extension and they offer to transfer you, ask for the number you are being transferred to in case you get disconnected.

Write down the time and date that you left a message so you can call back at an appropriate time if you don't get a return call.

When leaving a message with someone, ask for that person's name.

Ask if there is a direct line to the extension so you can skip the telephone menu.

If you have call-waiting, shut if off while making important calls, unless you are waiting for a crucial telephone call.

Networking Do's and Don'ts

Don't be afraid to test new waters or ask for help.

Don't be afraid to voice disagreements with professionals.

Don't hesitate to seek second opinions.

Don't be afraid to ask someone to accompany you to a core meeting.

Don't panic until you get all the facts.

Don't get locked into a dead-end feeling, there are always little roads intertwined.

Do talk to other parents and join organizations.

Do raise questions and concerns.

Do practice being an active decision maker.

Do learn the special education process and vocabulary words.

Do gather as much information as possible from every source possible.

Do know your legal rights.

Do stay in touch with the school, teacher, principal, and guidance counselor.

Chapter 4: Advocacy

Advocacy is "providing support."

An advocate is the one who pleads the cause of another.

Many formal advocacy groups exist such as the National Associations for Retarded Citizens (NARC) and the Learning Disabilities Association (LDA).

Focus efforts on state and federal legislation.

Parents must be advocates for a child's development and education—studies show children do better in school when parents are involved, particularly in special education.

Parents need as much information as possible by reading literature in the field and talking to other parents.

Join a local parent support group, or start one.

Know your legal rights.

Contact the special education office for available programs.

Invite professionals to come to the IEP meeting with you.

Maintain regular contact with your child's teacher.

Follow through on all leads.

Stand up for your child and fight on his or her behalf when necessary.

Chapter 5: The Special Needs Child in the Medical World

Before the Appointment

Try to keep the home atmosphere as close to routine as possible, to provide a sense of security and stability.

Avoid whispering in front of the child/children.

Let children know what is happening, at age-appropriate levels, with clear, honest, and simple facts.

Take care of the special sibling:

- Make sure his activities are taken care of too.
- Let him know what is happening.
- Let him help in as much decision making as possible.
- If you can't make other arrangements for the sibling's activities, try not to have a tight schedule between the appointment and the activity.
- If appropriate, have the sibling join you on appointments and therapies.

Call ahead for directions, ask for parking availability, ask what floor the office is on.

Leave plenty of time to get there.

Take the telephone number with you in case you need to call.

During the Appointment

Be prepared with activities and food for all those attending the appointment, and a favorite toy or doll, if age-appropriate.

Keep a doctor's notebook, with a copy at home. Keep telephone numbers, addresses, secretary's names, specialist, who referred you.

Keep a notebook to write down any questions you want to ask, and take notes at the appointment.

Make sure you allow the special needs child and/or the special sibling to ask any questions.

After the Appointment

If you forget to ask anything at the appointment, call back and state what you forgot.

Discuss the appointment with the child at the appropriate time, including impending tests.

Keep track of future long-term appointments in your calendar.

Don't be afraid to seek second opinions.

Look into all options.

The Hospital Stay

Prepare a child for hospitalization by providing them with information at their level. A professional can help you with ideas or strategies.

Chapter 6: The Special Needs Child in Education

Know the current state and federal laws and regulations regarding referral, identification, placement, and services.

Consult legal experts if needed.

Contact the State Department of Education and federal government to request information.

Early Intervention

Contact an Early Intervention Team if your child is between birth and three years of age and you suspect a problem.

After Starting School

Teacher, parent, or professional can request a referral for evaluation at any stage of the education process.

Parental consent is required before an evaluation can be made.

Parents must be notified of decision if it is decided by the evaluation team that an evaluation is not warranted.

Parents may contest this decision.

Schools must send notifications to parents regarding initiation or refusal of services and those notices must provide parents with some specific and detailed information.

Make the child aware of the impending evaluation and give him or her reassurance about it.

A social history or home assessment may be completed.

Once an evaluation has been completed, the evaluation team will determine if a child is eligible for special education, and if so, an IEP meeting must be scheduled.

Procedural Safeguards

Safety nets to make sure parents are involved in decisions made on behalf of the child.

Parents need to familiarize themselves with the safeguards.

Preparing for an Evaluation

The child should be told of the evaluation by the parents.

Explain to the child the purpose of the evaluation.

Tell the child who will come to see him and that they will ask him to do different activities.

Reassure the child that he is not expected to complete all the tasks during the evaluation.

Expect a social history or home assessment by a school social worker.

Upon completion the evaluation team will determine if a child is eligible for special education.

Preparing for the IEP meeting

Speak to other parents.

Make notes of questions you want to ask.

Bring anyone you want, professional or not.

Bring pencil and paper for taking notes.

Ask to see evaluations prior to the meeting if they are available.

Take a list of your child's strengths and weaknesses.

Know your child's goals.

The IEP Meeting

There is a federal minimum of who is required to attend.

IEP must be developed before the child can receive services.

IEP must be put into effect as soon as possible after the IEP meeting.

There is a legal obligation to provide services . . . listed in the IEP.

Parents must be an active part in forming the IEP.

School must provide the least restrictive environment for your child.

Parents should request a copy of the evaluations and the IEP.

Look at emotional and social factors affecting the child in the educational world.

If parents and school disagree, original IEP stays in place until the new one is decided.

Try to resolve differences through due process procedures, develop an interim program, and use mediation to resolve issues.

Parents can request a hearing if necessary.

After the IEP Meeting

If you forgot to ask questions during the IEP meeting, call back—it's never too late.

Always know who your contact person is.

You can request an independent evaluation if you disagree with the school's findings, at the school's expense.

Transition services information is also included in the IEP, no later than by the time the child is sixteen years of age.

IEP is a not a guarantee that the child will progress at a given rate.

Annual evaluations of the child are required by law.

A three-year re-evaluation is also required by law.

Keep the lines of communication open between you and the school.

Touch base frequently with the teacher, so he or she has a complete picture of your child.

Clarify homework expectations from the school.

Give feedback to teachers on the positives as well as negatives.

Parents can request an IEP meeting to be reconvened at any time.

Try to be preventive in averting issues; early intervention is better than crisis intervention.

Parents can request to examine their child's records, can ask for amendments if there is something inaccurate, and can include a written statement in the report about the discrepancy in the information.

Parental consent is required before anyone outside the school can examine the records.

Independent Evaluations

An independent evaluation is performed by a qualified professional who is not a member of the school's evaluation team.

Parents have the right to request an independent evaluation at the school's expense if they do not agree with the school's assessment.

Parents have the right to have an independent evaluation at their own expense.

Results from an independent evaluation must be considered in the development of a child's IEP.

Find out time line requirements from your state for requesting an independent evaluation.

Find out and carefully follow the procedures that apply to your school system if you want the independent evaluation done at public expense.

Chapter 7: Transitions

We are constantly facing and negotiating transitions in our daily living.

The level of transitioning varies for everyone; what is small for some can be monumental for others.

You need ongoing support and understanding.

You need time and space to reacquaint yourselves.

The child himself doesn't always recognize the transitioning problem—you must be on top of it.

A child's negative behavior can be a manifestation of transitioning difficulty.

Be prepared to allot adequate time in advance for transitions.

Constant negotiation of transitions is a requirement in our daily living and affects people differently—what may be small for some can be monumental for others.

Ongoing need for support and understanding from friends and family.

Give yourself and others time and space to get used to the changes.

Keep in mind that a child may manifest bad behavior as a reaction to a transition without recognizing the cause. Help him to understand.

Prepare in advance for transitions.

Chapter 8: Support Systems

Seeking and accessing support services is a sign of strength.

Support system is a term not only refering to help provided by the immediate family, but also to friends, professionals, and special organizations. They all can share the task of nurturing and educating the special needs child.

By seeking support for yourself you indirectly help your child.

Build a broad support base, so if you lose one the others will be there.

Teach your child how to recognize and use support systems for themselves. This helps foster independence in the child.

Chapter 9: Special Siblings, Special Parents

The parent is the ultimate advocate regardless of the situation.

Remember we are dealing with more than the special needs child. We have the special parent, the special sibling, the special friend, the special family as a whole.

Significant people outside the family will play an important role in helping the child with special needs face his or her difficulties. These other people can be very influential in the development of the child's self-esteem, confidence, and outlook on life.

These significant others also will be touched by their interactions and experiences with the special needs child.

Chapter 10: Things We Never Even Thought About

Being as prepared as possible when the unexpected arrives can alleviate much anxiety.

Driving

Handicapped automobiles are available for driving.

Traveling with a Special Needs Child

Ask for a hotel room near the elevator, an aisle seat, or anything close that will help with walking, if that is an issue.

Don't be afraid to make your needs known.

Keep a log of the questions you have asked so you will remember in the future.

Sexuality

Look for books and organizations to assist you in this area.

When the Doctor Moves or Retires

If the doctor moves, and it is feasible, follow him; if this is impossible or the doctor retires, consider his recommendations regarding replacements.

Moving away with a Special Needs Child

Utilize the resources in that city, state, or country that deal with special education, organizations in the telephone book—put those networking skills to use!

Money Management

A small bank account with little funds or a credit card with limited funds can be a solution to children seeking independence and being concerned with money problems.

Be on guard for your child agreeing to any unwanted solicitations.

Other Illness in the Family

Use respite to refuel yourself for the strength to cope with the other illness.

Try to put support systems in place as quickly as possible.

Parents Aging or Dying

Put future plans into action now; whether considering respite care, residential schools, institutions, residential/ community homes, private residential, or relatives. Look at these facilities now or at least be aware of the options.

Socialization

Take the initiative if necessary and look for social organizations, such as Big Brother/Big Sister, or more casual play groups.

After-School Care

You might have to contact organizations on an individual basis if this is not available or appropriate at the current school.

A nonacademic setting can enhance other skills.

Religious Rites of Passage

Remember that your child might experience this in a slightly different fashion or a modified fashion. Celebrate!

Dietary Restrictions

Obtain as many products as necessary for that particular need and keep a list.

Always leave a number where you can be reached so any questions concerning food can be asked.

Housing

Talk to a lawyer about guardianship and seek options there as well.

Look at all possibilities, from independent to umbrella situations, depending on needs.

Occupation

Some doors will be opened and others will be closed; remember, there are many facilities to help you with this.

Workplaces do offer special programs for the special needs individual.

Humor

Try not to lose your sense of humor.

Don't be afraid to laugh—laughter is good.

12

Conclusion: Special Outlook

In writing this book, we have shared our special outlook on what parents need to know to prepare themselves to assist with their special needs child. We have tried to give you the necessary information and tools in helping your special needs child, from informative definitions to available resources and techniques for networking. Obtaining this knowledge is just one step in the process; keeping the momentum going is the more crucial element.

It is easy to absorb the information, process it in our minds, and head out full force on the path to "conquer the world" and try to solve or at least deal with all your child's special needs. But to maintain this momentum is an ongoing task, one that takes a lot of energy, both emotionally and physically. You must pace yourself, and you must not exert all your energies at once and be exhausted so that you are not able to move forward. Sometimes more than others, your total and ongoing attention may be demanded. Sometimes your special needs child requires an all-consuming few days, weeks, or longer, but you need to recognize when this demand tapers off, for it would be most difficult to keep this kind of pace in the long run. Recognizing the lulls and learning to pace ourselves thus becomes necessary in order to remain energetic and productive.

There is also the temptation of falling into a false sense of security if your child is at a stage where he is doing well and there are no rough waves to ride. Your child is making progress and the necessary supports are in place. You have embarked wholeheartedly in seeking the services and support needed by your child, and you are now enjoying the fruits of your labor. Savor that time, but always remain observant, prepared, and guarded for what may come your way. Often, these quiet times are followed by periods requiring that once again you go full force and gear up for a new stage, transition, or issue that your child is facing. Nothing is guaranteed in life, and these guarantees when dealing with a special needs child waiver even more. Nothing remains static. If your child regresses or hits some bumps in the road, it does not necessarily indicate some failure on your part, or the child's, or the teacher's, or whoever is involved with your child. It just means that there are some extra challenges.

It sometimes might be difficult to get this momentum going again. You must remember, though, that whenever you start a task or reengage in something, the beginning can be difficult, even frightening, but you must also keep in mind that the skills you have learned and used in the past are there and will help you to get going again. And just because a new agenda, one that requires additional attention, is put in your path does not mean starting from scratch. Experiencing life with your child and reading this book has equipped you with the tools and knowledge that will assist you to properly channel your energy and catapult you into action. You have been networking, collecting resources, building blocks—call on these as you move along. Now, you are no longer a novice. Having your records up to date and your file systems organized will strengthen you and prepare you for the unexpected twists and turns, thus allowing you to once again re-engage and keep the momentum going.

You have the tools, you know to keep up the momentum—now what? Where do you go from here? Outlook means having a prospect for the future, having a point of view. Make sure to take time to think about this. Understanding your child's special needs and accessing services and supports can be a consuming process, a full-time job in certain cases. It is easy to get so involved in the process that you lose sight of other important things in your life. Remember that your child is more than his special need. See him as a whole entity. Enjoy your child, meet the challenges and then celebrate the victories and milestones with your child, family, and others.

It is also important to make room to pursue personal interests. Don't cut yourself off from the outside world and curtail yourself to being a parent and advocate of a child with special needs. Finding this harmonious balance between parenthood and selfhood is not necessarily easy, but it is not impossible.

In concluding this book for special needs parents, we find it is difficult to bring it to a close, because there are always ongoing transitions and challenges. Life is ongoing, and life is one transition after another. As our children grow up, their needs may increase or decrease, requiring us to adjust and re-evaluate our course of action. The laws and regulations can change or be amended, reflecting the social, political, and economic climate of our times. New programs, services, and therapies might be developed, providing us with a wider range of options to consider. The field of special education has undergone changes over the years and is bound to continue. There have been gains, but at times, parents have encountered situations that have required them to question or challenge the system.

Thus, our goal has been to equip you with skills and reassure you that all parents can successfully advocate on their child's behalf. As stated earlier, all of the skills we present in our book can be learned. In addition, numerous organizations, books, and services can provide parents with additional information, support, and guidance. Accept the challenge of your special assignment, conquer the maze, toss out that net, and know in your heart that you have had, and will continue to have, the courage and strength to enhance your child's life and future. You are a fighter and survivor—so is your special needs child.

If we can leave you with one last thought, remember that your special needs child is a child. Think of your child as the ultimate in art, perfectly orchestrated with distinct lines and brilliant colors. Your special needs child is the perfect picture, just looked at from an angle different than the rest of the world.

Glossary

Academic Aide   A person assigned to assist the special needs student with academic tasks in the classroom.

Access Rights   Each participating agency shall permit parents to inspect and review any educational records relating to their children that are collected, maintained, or used by the agency. The agency shall comply with a request without unnecessary delay and before any meeting regarding an individualized educational program or hearing relating to the identification, evaluation, or placement of the child. Time lines vary from state to state.

Advocate   A person chosen or hired by the parent to help the parent access needed services and/or programs for the special needs child. The advocate can also help with the appeals process.

Appeals Process   If the school or parents disagree with the decisions reached at a due process hearing, they can request that the case be heard again at a higher court.

Assessment   Testing or observation that is done in order to describe the abilities of the child. This can be done in the educational, psychological, developmental, as well as medical areas, including, speech, hearing, etc.

Categories   Students who have special needs are grouped together because of shared characteristics. The names and definitions that are assigned to the categories vary from state to state.

Children with Disabilities   Those children identified in accordance with Regulations 300.530-300.534 as being mentally retarded, hard of hearing, deaf, speech-impaired, visually handicapped, seriously emotionally disturbed, orthopedically impaired, other health-impaired, deaf-blind, multihandicapped, or having specific learning disabilities, who because of those impairments need special education and related services.

Clinical Social Workers   A professional with a master's degree in social work, with some states requiring a license and others requiring registration. Must have a minimum of two years of supervised experience.

Consent   The parent has been fully informed of the compulsory information in his or her native language, or in writing or other appropriate means of communication; and the parent understands and agrees in writing. Consent is voluntary and can be revoked at any time.

Continuum of Alternative Placements   A selection of alternative placements when deciding on a child's placement in special education. The services can range from the most restrictive placement to the least restrictive placement.

Disability   A difficulty caused by medical, social, or learning factors that affects the normal development or functioning of an individual.

Due Process   The legal procedures that provide an individual with protection of his or her constitutional rights.

Due Process Hearing   When schools and parents cannot resolve a dispute over a child's identification of special needs or the educational program for the child, either party can request a hearing. A hearing is a formal meeting, presided over by a hearing officer who follows most rules of evidence. Detailed briefs are presented, and these meetings can vary in length depending on the state.

Early Intervention   A service for children and their families that provides educational, therapeutic, and support services for children from birth to age three, who are either at risk for delay in development or are currently displaying delays.

Educational Objectives   When a child has been evaluated, these are the goals stated in the IEP that the child will be working toward and the skills to be accomplished.

Eligibility   The term used when a child is determined to be in need of special needs services.

Enrichment   Materials and activities that help enhance the child's curriculum but do not affect a student's placement.

Evaluation   Procedures used to determine whether a child is handicapped and the nature and extent of the special education and related services that the child needs. This will determine whether the child is eligible for special education and to be put on an individualized education plan (IEP).

Evaluation Team   An evaluation is performed by a group of professionals, including teachers, psychologists, and other pertinent specialists who are qualified to administer assessments providing information on the disability of the child. This team is also involved in making recommendations regarding placement and services needed for the appropriate education of a child with special needs.

Evaluation Team Meeting   A meeting to discuss the findings of the assessments once an evaluation has been completed. The evaluation team is responsible for determining if a child is eligible for special education.

FAPE (Free Appropriate Public Education)   Special education and related services provided at public expense, under public supervision and direction, and without charge. They must meet the state education standards. FAPE runs from preschool through secondary education. It strives to place the child with special needs in the least restrictive environment.

Fine Motor Activities   Skills that require fine coordination for small movements such as handwriting, sewing, and buttoning.

Gross Motor Activities   Activities that involve the major muscle groups, i.e., walking, going from sitting to standing, rolling.

Guidance Counselor   The professional that provides students with advice on educational or vocational issues as well as social difficulties.

IDEA (Individuals with Disabilities Education Act)   An amendment of the Education of All Handicapped Children

Act, which also includes a definition of transition services and specifies what needs to be included in individualized transition plans.

IEP (Individualized Education Plan)   A written document developed at an individualized education plan meeting, indicating the special needs of a child, the educational services and support services that he or she is to receive, the educational goals and objectives, and other pertinent information required for the development and implementation of the child's educational program.

IEP Meeting   A meeting to develop the individualized education plan for a child with special needs, taking into consideration the recommendations of the evaluation team and input from the child's teachers and parents. Placement decisions for the child are made at this time.

IFSP (Individualized Family Service Plan)   Term applicable only for children in early intervention programs. The IFSP is a written document that specifies the following: the present level of development of the child and the needs of the family as they relate to the needs of the child; the objectives and specific services for the child and the family, procedures for evaluation, and procedures for transitioning from early intervention programs to the preschool programs.

Inclusion   Providing the special needs student with the opportunity to receive his or her education in the regular classroom setting despite the type or severity of the disability.

Independent Education Evaluation   An evaluation conducted by a qualified examiner not employed by the public agency responsible for the education of the child in question.

ITP (Individualized Transition Plan)   This is a part of the IEP that states the services needed by a student with special needs in order to transition from school to post-school activities, such as postsecondary education, vocational training, integrated employment, continuing and adult education, adult services, independent living, or community participation.

Law   A rule recognized as binding or enforced by a controlling authority that requires obedience.

Mainstream   Providing special needs children the opportunity to interact and be educated with nonspecial needs children to the maximum possibility.

Mediation   When there is a dispute between the school and the parents over the child's identification or educational program, mediation is one of the available steps that allows both parties to review and discuss the problem. Through this dialogue, alternative solutions to the problem are explored, often leading to a resolution. This is a voluntary process, and it is not binding.

Mobility Aide   An individual assigned to assist a student in the school setting to move from one place to another and provide safety of movement for that student.

Nonacademic Services   Services that include counseling, athletics, transportation, health services, and recreational activities.

Occupational Therapy   Therapy conducted through a series of activities that promotes recovery or rehabilitation. Adaptive living skills are also enhanced and taught.

PAC (Parent Advisory Council)   These groups meet on a regular (usually monthly) basis to discuss parents' concerns with the special education programs, to invite speakers in the field, and to provide parents with an opportunity to meet other parents in the school district, keeping them abreast of changes, issues, and other relevant information.

Parent   A parent, guardian, or surrogate parent, who has been appointed in accordance with Regulation 300.514. The state is not included in this term if the child is a ward of the state.

Parent Participation   When parents are permitted active and equal participation in discussing and developing an individualized education plan and in providing input regarding their child's educational programming process.

Physical Therapy   Treatment that involves physical and mechanical means, such as massage, water, exercise, heat, etc.

Policies   The methods of actions that are established at the local level by the board of education. The board of education is responsible for the direct delivery of special education services in its area. Its policies will reflect state laws and regulations.

Pre-Referral Intervention   Prior to making a referral to special education, this is the process by which the teachers try to identify different means of assisting and resolving the student's difficulties within the regular classroom setting and of accessing other available resources in the system outside of special education.

Procedural Safeguards   The safety nets built into the law to make sure that parents are involved in decisions being made on behalf of the child with special needs.

Psychiatrist   A physician that specializes in mental, emotional, or behavioral disorders. A psychiatrist can dispense medication.

Psychologist   A specialist in the science of mind and behavior. A psychologist cannot dispense medication.

Public Agency   This includes the state educational agency, local educational agencies, intermediate educational units, and any other political subdivisions of the state responsible for providing education to handicapped children.

Public Expense   (Evaluation at the Public Expense) When the public agency either pays for the full cost of the evaluation or ensures that the evaluation is otherwise provided at no cost to the parent.

Qualified   A person has met state educational agency-approved or -recognized certification, licensing, registration, or other comparable requirements that apply to the area in which he or she is providing special education or related services.

Reevaluation of the IEP   Every three years, a child's IEP must be reevaluated to update the present educational plan and ensure that the services and goals are appropriate and reflect the present educational needs and support required by the child.

Referral   The first step that is taken when a parent, teacher, or other professional is concerned with the possibility of a child having a disability. Through this process, the evaluating team in a school will decide if the child should be evaluated for eligibility for special education services.

Regulations Once laws are passed, these describe the procedures that need to be followed in order to comply with the law.

Related Services Transportation and other such developmental, corrective, and other supportive services as are required to assist a child with disabilities to benefit from special education, including speech pathology, audiology, psychological services, physical and occupational therapy, recreation, early identification and assessment of disabilities in children, counseling services, and medical services for diagnostic or evaluation purposes. The term also includes school health services, social work services in schools, and parent counseling and training.

Respite Care Care given by an individual or an organization to provide temporary relief of the caretaking responsibilities for the parents of the special needs child.

Review of IEP Every year, a child's IEP is reviewed to see what progress the child has made, where he or she continues to need support, and what type of support.

Separate Classes The classroom that houses only the special needs children with a teacher certified in special education who has primary responsibility for the educational plan.

Special Education Specifically designed instruction, at no cost to the parent, to meet the unique needs of a handicapped child, including classroom instruction, instruction in physical education, home instruction, and instruction in hospitals and institutions.

Special Needs   Although it is assumed that special needs refers specifically to children with academic challenges or learning difficulties, these are just two of the categories that fall under the term. Also included in this list of special needs is the gifted child.

Surrogate Parent   An individual assigned by a public agency to act as a surrogate for the parents when no parents can be identified, when the whereabouts of a parent can't be discovered, or when a child is a ward of the state. The surrogate may represent the child in all matters relating to: 1) identification, evaluation, and educational placement of the child and 2) the provision of a free and appropriate public education to the child.

Transition   The change from one place, stage, or activity to another, including school to school and school to post-school activities.

Vocational Education   Organized educational programs that are directly related to the preparation of individuals for paid or unpaid employment or for additional preparation for a career requiring other than a baccalaureate or advanced degree.

Index

A

Advocacy
  attention deficit disorder children, 189–190
  classroom observations for, 60–64
  definition, 53, 232–233
  groups, 54
  in IEP meetings, 59–60
  networking and, 57
  residential care, 193–194
  resources for, 56–58, 232–233
  services, 116
  for special education, 54–64
After-school programs, 221–222, 242
Answering machines, 18–19
Appeals
  to IEPs, 98–100
    federal regulations governing, 100–101
    mediation, 101

Appointments, see Doctor appointments
Attention deficit disorder children, 177–191
  advocacy for, 189–190
  college and, 184
  color sensitivity in, 182
  networking with other parents, 181–182
  parents with, survival strategies, 186–188
  support groups, 177–179, 181–182
  transitions and, 184–185

B

Beepers, 17–18

C

Calendars, using efficiently, 26–27, 229

Call waiting, 21

Carphones, 23, *see also* Telephones

Children, *see* Special needs children

Classroom, observations, importance in advocacy, 60–64

College
attention deficit disorder children and, 184
gaining admission to, students concern with, 148–149

Color sensitivity
in attention deficit disorder children, 182

Computers, 22

Confidentiality
child's right of, 165
records and, 16, 112–114

Consent
parental, in IEPs, 88
special education records, 113

Copy machine, 16

D

Death
of doctor, 210–212
of parent, 219–220, 242
financial aspects, 219–220
of support system member, 169–170

Diagnosis, parental acceptance of, 4–6

Dietary restrictions, 222–223, 243

Divorce, effects on special needs child, 198–199

Doctor, death of, 210–212

Doctor appointments, 66–67, 234
follow-ups, 77–78
including siblings, 69–70

involving child, 67, 75, 77
preparing for, 70–73, 233
questions, 74–76
reviewing, 76, 234
scheduling, 69
second opinions, 78–79

Driving, with special needs child, 206–207, 240

E

Early interventions
eligibility, 129
parents role, 130–131, 138–139
private preschool director and teacher on, 136–139
public nursery, evaluating, 134–135
referrals for, 129
special program coordinator interview on, 129–132
timing, 131
transition to preschool, 133–139

Education, *see* Special education

Elementary school
transitions, 139–140
preparation, 142

Evaluations, *see also* Independent evaluations
for special education, 91–92, 236

F

Fax machines, 22–23

Federal regulations
for appealing IEP decisions, 100–101
for developing and revising IEPs, 93–95

for IEP meetings, 87–89
for independent evaluations,
  103–104
for special education, 86,
  90–91

G

Goal setting, in special education, 111–112
Guardianship, 151–155
  advantages, 152–153, 154
  initiating, 154–155
  lawyer interview on, 151–155
  limited, 153–154
    definition, 153
Guidance counselors
  communication with, 109
  parents, assistance to, 149
  student, assistance to, 150
  transition, assistance in,
    150–151
Guilt, overcoming, 6–7

H

Hemingway, Ernest, 52
High school
  guidance counselor, interview,
    147–150
  transitions, 143–144
    parents needs, 147–148
    parents role, 145–147
    preparation, 144
    students concerns, 148–149
Homework, parent's participation in, 106–107
Hospitalization, preparation,
  81–82, 234
Housings, for adult special needs
  children, 223, 243

Humor, importance of,
  224–225, 243

I

IEP, *see* Individualized education
  plan
Illness, in other family members,
  217–218, 242
Independent evaluations, *see also*
  Evaluations
  federal regulations governing,
    103–104
  for IEP, 96, 238
Individualized education plan (IEP),
  see also Special education
  appealing decisions, 98–100,
    98–101
  development and revisions,
    93–95, 96–98
  independent evaluations, 96
  meetings
    advocacy in, 59–60, 236–238
    evaluating, 102
    federal regulations govern-
      ing, 87–89, 95–96
  parental consent in, 88
  preparing for, 94–95
  procedural safeguards, 89–90,
    235–236
  transition services in, 96,
    104–105
  updating, 105–106
Interventions, *see* Early
  interventions
Interviews
  children in residential setting,
    mothers with, 191–193
  director and teacher of private
    preschool program,
    136–139

Interviews, *continued*
director of public preschool
program, 133–139
divorce and special needs
child, 198–199
early interventions, special
program coordinator on,
129–132
four special needs children,
mother with, 194–196
guardianship, lawyer on,
151–155
high school guidance counselor, 147–150
learning disabled child,
mother with, 176–177
medical and learning special
needs child, mother with,
200–202
secondary education, 143–147
special program coordinator on
early intervention, 129–132
transitions, elementary school
psychologist and social
worker on, 139–143
transitions, social worker on,
123–129

K

Key elements, 227–243

L

Lawyer, on guardianship, inter-
view, 151–155
Learning Disabilities Association
(LDA), 54
Learning disabled child, interview
with mother of, 176–177
Legal services, 116

M

Mediation, in IEP disputes, 101
Medical, *see* Doctor appointments; Hospitalization
Middle school
transitions, 140–141
preparations, 142
Money
death of parent and, 219–220
management, 216–217, 241
Mothers, *see also* Parents
with attention deficit disorder
child, 177–191
with children in residential
setting, 191–193
with four special needs children, 194–196
with learning disabled child,
176–177
with a medical and learning
special needs child,
200–202
with specical needs child,
effects of divorce, 198–199
Moving, 212–216, 241

N

National Association for Retarded Citizens (NARC), 54
Networking
advocacy and, 57
definition, 33
gathering information by, 41–42
newspapers for, 50
with organizations, 42–43
with other special needs
parents, 44–45
parents with attention deficit
disorder children,
181–182, 189–190

requesting assistance, 39–41
role in transition, 51
rules of, 34–36, 230
telephones in, 45–50, 231
tools, 37–38
transitions and, 159
Newspapers, for networking, 50

O

Occupation, for special needs
children, 223–224, 243
Office of Special Education
Programs, 86
Organizations, networking with,
42–43
Organization skills
in coping with attention deficit
disorder child, 179
equipment for, 16–23, 229
answering machines, 18–19
beepers, 17–19
call waiting, 21
computers, 22
copy machines, 16
fax machines, 22–23
filing systems, 14–15
keeping copies, 15–16, 228
postal supplies, 24
record keeping, 13, 228
teaching children about, 31
time management, 29–31, 230
using calenders efficiently,
26–27
using phone books efficiently,
24–26

P

Parent Advisor Council
(PAC), 58

Parents, *see also* Mothers
acceptance of diagnosis, 4–6
after-school programs and, 222
assisting in transitions,
123–126
with attention deficit disorder
children, 177–179,
180–181
networking, 181–182
communication
guidance counselors, 109
teachers, 107–109, 110–111
consent, 88
death of, 218–219, 242
financial aspects, 219–220
early interventions, role in,
130–131, 134–135,
138–139
elementary and middle school
transitions, role in,
139–141
guidance counselor, assistance
to, 149
high school transitions,
145–147, 147–148
homework, participation in,
106–107
prioritizing responsibilities,
6–7
problems faced by, 3–4
in special education, ongoing
role, 106–116
transitions, role in, 161
Physical therapy, *see* Therapy
Preschool, *see* Early interventions
Preschool directors
private, early intervention
interview, 136–139
public, early intervention
interview, 133–139

Procedural safeguards
in IEP meetings, 89–90
Psychologist
elementary and middle school
transitions, interview,
139–143

R

Records
confidentiality of, 16,
112–114
Religious rites of passage,
222, 242
Residential care
advocacy, 193–194
children in, mother's with,
191–193
effect on siblings, 191–192
parental survival strategies for,
191–192

S

School, *see* Special education
Secondary education
interviews on, 143–147
Sexuality
special needs child and, 210
Siblings
involvement with special needs
child
doctor appointments, 68–69
therapy, 83–84
residential care for special
needs child, effects on,
191–192
and special needs child,
173–175
Socialization, and special needs
child, 220–221

Social worker
elementary and middle school
transitions, interview,
139–143
transitions, interview, 123–129
Special education, *see also*
Individualized education
plan (IEP)
accessing
preparation, 85
advocacy in, 54–64
communication with teachers,
107–109, 110–111
early intervention, 87, 235
evaluations, 91–92
federal regulations, 86, 90–91
goal setting, 111–112
guidance counselors, 109
ongoing parental involvement,
106–116, 235
records, confidentiality and,
112–114
role in transitions, 126–127
Special needs
definition, 1–2
Special needs children, *see also*
Students
after school programs,
221–222
attention deficit disorder,
interview with mother,
177–191
death of doctor and,
210–212, 241
death of support system member, 169–170
dietary restrictions, 222–223
doctor appointments, involving in, 67, 75, 77
driving with, 206–207, 241
effects of divorce, 198–199

housing and, 223
illness in other family members and, 217–218
learning disabled, interview with mother with, 176–177
with medical problems, interview of mother with, 200–202
mother with four, interview, 194–196
moving to new town, 212–216, 241
occupations for, 223–224
and sexuality, 210, 241
sibling involvement with, 68–69, 83–84
and socialization, 220–221, 242
support systems for, 163–170
teaching organization strategies to, 31
transitions, anxiety over, 159–161
travel with, 207–210, 241
Special program coordinator
early intervention interview, 129–132
Speech therapy, *see* Therapy
Students, *see also* Special needs children
college admission, concerns with, 148–149
high school transitions, concerns with, 148–149
Support groups
attention deficit disorder children, parents with, 181–182, 183–184
for coping with attention deficit disorder child, 177

Support systems
for child, 163–170, 240
accessing, 166–167
importance of confidentiality, 165
multiple, importance of, 168–170
for parents, 170–171, 240

T

Teachers
communication with, 107–109, 110–111
goal setting with, 111–112
private preschool, on preschool transitioning, 136–139
Telephone books
updating, importance of, 25–26
using efficiently, 24–25
Telephones, *see also* Carphones
in networking, 45–50, 231
Therapy, 82–84
for coping with attention deficit disorder child, 177–178
including siblings, 83
Time management, 29–31
Transition meetings, 158–159
Transitions
adjusting to, difficulty, 128, 239
after early interventions, 129
age-related difficulties, 125–126
assisting in, 123–126
attention deficit disorder child and, 179–180, 184–185
child's anxiety over, 159–161

Transitions, *continued*
  common needs, 124–124
  in daily life, 118–120
  strategies for, 120–121
  elementary and middle school
    transitions, 142
  elementary school, 139–140
  high school, 143–144
    parents role, 145–148
    preparation, 144
    students concerns, 148–149
  introduction, 117–118
  major, introduction, 121–123
  major issues in, 131–132, 239
  middle school, 140–141
  moving away, 212–216
  networking and, 51, 159
  new doctor, 210–212
  parent's role in, 161
  preparation, 157–158
  preschool, 133–136

  private preschool director and
    teacher on, 136–139
  problems in, determining,
    137–138
  public to private school,
    128–129
  school's role in, 126–127
  social worker interview on,
    123–129
Transition services
  in IEP, 104, 104–105
  requirements for, 96
Travel, with special needs child,
  207–210, 241

W

Wards
  definition, 152
  rights of, 153

Laws and Resources

We have endeavored to highlight various laws and resources for you. Some of these resources are associations that you can join and get on their mailing lists and subscribe to newsletters. We have tried to give a broad overview of the various councils, associations, and organizations that are available. Fees vary from organization to organization and the best advice we can offer is to call or write to them for more information.

There are both federal and state organizations. To locate them, look in the government section of your telephone book. You can also telephone the federal government information line and explain what your needs are. Each state also has a department of education for special needs.

Laws and Amendments of Importance for Special Education

Section 504 of the Vocational Rehabilitation Act PL. 93-112 (1973)

PL. 94-142 (1975)	The education for all handicapped children act (ages 3–21)
PL. 99-457 (1986)	Amendment to the education for all handicapped children act. Extended rights and protection of the law to include infants and toddlers

PL. 101-476 (1990)   The education of the handicapped act amendment and renamed it as the individual with disabilities education act (IDEA)

PL. 101-336 (1990)   The American with Disabilities Act (ADA)

Resources

Many resources distribute pamphlets and information. Some are free and some are available for a small fee. The best thing to do is write or call for more details.

To Obtain a Copy of the Federal Regulations for Special Education, Write or Call:

Federal Regulations for Special Education
State Department of Education *or*
Office of Special Education Programs
Department of Education
400 Maryland Avenue, SW
Washington, DC 20202
(202) 205-8825
(202) 205-9090 deaf or hearing impaired

Alexander Graham Bell Association for the Deaf (AGBAD)
3417 Volta Place, NW
Washington, DC 20007

American Alliance for Health, Physical Education, Recreation and Dance (AAHPERD)
P.O. Box 10375
Alexandria, VA 22310

American Association of University Affiliated Programs for Persons with Developmental Disabilities (AAUAP)
8605 Cameron Street, Suite 406
Silver Springs, MD 20910

American Camp Associations
206 Moody Street
Waltham, MA 02154
(617) 899-2042

American Council of the Blind (ACB)
1010 Vermont Avenue, NW, Suite 1100
Washington, DC 20005

American Orthopsychiatric Association (AOA)
19 West 44th Street Suite 1616
New York, NY 10036

American Speech/Language/Hearing Association (ASHA)
10801 Rockville Pike
Rockville, MD 20852-3279

Association on Higher Education and Disability (AHEAD)
P.O. Box 21192
Columbus, OH 43221
(800) 247-7752

The Association for the Care of Children's Health (ACCH)
7910 Woodmont Avenue, Suite 300
Bethesda, MD 20814

Association for Persons in Supported Employment (APSE)
P.O. Box 27523
Richmond, VA 23261-7523

The Association for Retarded Citizens (ARC)
2501 Avenue J
Arlington, TX 76011

Autism Society of America (ASA)
8601 Georgia Avenue, Suite 503
Silver Springs, MD 20901

Clearing House on Disability Information
Office of Special Education and Rehabilitative Services (OSERS)
Room 3132, Switzer Building
330 C Street, SW
Washington, DC 20202-2524

Center for Minority Special Education (CMSE)
114 Phenix Hall
Hampton University
Hampton, VA 23668
(800) 241-1441

Council for Exceptional Children (CEC)
1920 Association Drive
Reston, VA 22091-1589

Direct Link for the Disabled, Inc.
P.O. Box 1036
Solvang, CA 93464
(805) 688-1603

Eric Clearing House on Adult, Career, and Vocational Education
Ohio State University
Center on Education and Training for Employment
1960 Kenny Road
Columbus, OH 43210-1090

Eric Clearing House on Handicapped and Gifted Children
Council for Exceptional Children
1920 Association Drive
Reston, VA 22091-1589

(Eric is a National Information System)

Federation for Children with Special Needs
95 Berkeley Street
Boston, MA 02116
(617) 482-2915

Learning Disabilities Association of America (LDA)
4156 Library Road
Pittsburgh, PA 15234

National Association for Gifted Children (NAGC)
5100 North Edgewood Drive
St. Paul, MN 55112

National Association of Protection and Advocacy Systems (NAPAS)
220 Eye Street, NE
Washington, DC 20202

National Coalition for Parent Involvement in Education (NCPIE)
1201 16th Street, NW, Room 810
Washington, DC 20036
(800) 999-5599